DARE TO
Dance
WITH HIM

PAULETTE ROLLE-ALESNIK

CREATION
HOUSE PRESS

DARE TO DANCE WITH HIM by Paulette Rolle-Alesnik
Published by Creation House Press
A Strang Company
600 Rinehart Road
Lake Mary, Florida 32746
www.creationhouse.com

Unless otherwise noted, all Scripture quotations are from the Holy Bible, New
International Version. Copyright © 1973, 1978, 1984, International Bible Society.
Used by permission.

Scripture quotations marked KJV are from the King James Version of the Bible.

Greek and Hebrew word definitions are from *The New Strong's Exhaustive
Concordance of the Bible Expanded Edition*, James Strong, ed. (Nashville, TN:
Thomas Nelson, 2001).

Word definitions marked *Webster's* are from *Webster's New World College
Dictionary*, fourth edition (New York: MacMillan, 1999).

This book is not intended to provide medical advice or to take the place of medical
advice and treatment from your personal physician. Readers are advised to consult
their own doctors or other qualified health professionals regarding the treatment
of their medical problems and before beginning any of the stretches or health suggestions in this book. Neither the publisher nor the author takes any responsibility
for any possible consequences from following the information in this book.

Cover design by Deion Gibson
Photographs by Joseph A. Alesnik
Interior design by Terry Clifton

Copyright © 2004 by Paulette Rolle-Alesnik
All rights reserved

Library of Congress Control Number: 2004109826
International Standard Book Number: 1-59185-645-0

04 05 06 07 08— 987654321
Printed in the United States of America

This book belongs in the hands of every true worshiper! Its contents minister to the whole man: spirit, soul, and body. It is a true reflection of 1 Thessalonians 5:23, "And may the God of peace Himself sanctify you through and through [separate you from profane things, make you pure and wholly consecrated to God] and may your spirit and soul and body be preserved sound and complete [and found] blameless at the coming of our Lord Jesus Christ (the Messiah)" (Amplified Bible). Those who read this book will be challenged to live an integrated and balanced life, always in His presence.

—REVEREND PAULINE "PAT" CLARK
WITHOUT WALLS INTERNATIONAL CHURCH

Dare to Dance With Him is unique in its contents. This book challenges you to use the physical, spiritual, mental, and emotional to establish a tangible relationship with the Lord of the Dance. Dancers, prepare your hearts to engage the presence of the Lord with the practical daily helps from scriptures to stretches and calling on His holy names. You too can move from a routine of worship to a lifestyle of worship dance.

—PASTORS JOE AND MARY BROWN
WORSHIP HIM HARVEST CHURCH INTERNATIONAL

DEDICATION

This book and its impact are dedicated to the One who made it all possible—my Father, the Lord Jesus Christ—and to those who dare to dance like no one's watching. For the dancer who desires growth inside and out, who desires to leap to new heights in Christ and in the dance, *you can make it*! As you go up, please take someone with you.

ACKNOWLEDGMENTS

Above all in heaven and earth, I thank my heavenly Father, Creator, Savior, and Friend—Jesus/Yeshua. I thank Him for the awesome opportunity to live in this era and for the "out of this world" idea for this book.

First and foremost I thank *my biggest supporter and number one fan*—my esteemed husband and friend, businessman Joseph A. Alesnik, who encourages me 150 percent to do all that is in my heart. Joe, you pressed me to complete and publish this book at all costs. You are always there, supporting and assisting me. I love you, Joe! A shout out to my dogs, Lord Pistol and Sir Cocoa, who stayed by my side countless hours as my Animal Kingdom Advisor Board and friends.

To my mom, Annie "A. J.," and the entire Rolle Family in the Bahamas, thank you for all you do. A. J. you are the "Queen Bee" of supporters. You are the backbone behind all of our successes. I love you, Mom.

To the MVPs (Most Valuable Pastors)—Pastors Randy and Paula White. Thank you for supporting what God has called me to do, and for praying, fasting, preaching, teaching, and encouraging me over the years. You always encouraged me to think BIG—to trust a big God, with a big promise, and a big vision! Through your persistent preaching, you have helped me realize that people are not my source—that God has a big plan for my life. For that I am eternally grateful. Thank you for inspiring me not to settle. Look at me now! Look at where God has brought me. I am going after all God has for me. Because of your teaching (in part), I will die empty of all God has deposited inside me! Thank you, pastors!

To a woman of God who has invested in me simply because she saw and experienced my passion for dancing—Naomi Lovett. You caught the vision and ran with it. You selflessly contributed many hours writing, suggesting, editing, rewriting, and creating my dream simply because you believed in me enough to *act*. Naomi, thank you for helping me write the original *Dare to Dance With Him* (which will be the manual to this book). My writer, friend, and prayer partner, thank you for your intercession, for having a heart of worship, and a heart after God. You were a big inspiration in getting this book done. *You were the wind beneath my wings*...thank you, friend, I love you Naomi. *You are my diamond.*

To the entire Without Walls International Church family, thank you for praying and ministering to Joe and me. Special thanks to the Fine Arts Department—especially the members (and former members) of Praise In Motion Dance Ministry and J.U.D.A.H Dance Company. Dancing with you is a joy. You are my inspiration to teach. Shout out to my colaborer in dance at Without Walls, D'Mario Henry. Thank you all for investing your time, prayers, words of encouragement, opportunities, smiles, and lots of love. I love you all.

To my mentors, Robert Allen and Mark Victor Hansen, who first inspired the idea and challenged me to write a book about anything I loved. When I thought I had nothing to say, you encouraged me to say it anyway—to leave a legacy of passion. Mark, you said the world was waiting for it. God used you to push me out of my comfort zone. You were right. Thank you for all the encouragement. Thanks to you, I have now written two books and there are a few more waiting inside of me.

To Dr. Sydel LeGrande, a powerful woman of God who has invested in me over the years. You have seen fit to invest in me once again. Thank you for assisting with verifying the health tips. Thank you for believing in me enough to *act* on it. I love you.

To the children and youth in my life who inspire me to leave this legacy. I enjoy watching you grow into passionate young adults. Thank you for showering me with love and for allowing me to teach you to dance. Special thanks to Imani LeGrande (the drama queen) and Charisma Donaldson (Ms. Compassion), former dance students. You girls tired me, but you always encouraged me to be kind. Never stop dancing. You, too, can do it!

To my eighth- and ninth-grade teacher, Mr. Lewis, who believed in me so much. You saw what others did not see. You encouraged my family to invest in honing my leadership skills. You once said to me on the steps of Georgetown Primary School (just before my speech completion), "Paulette, you can do this. You can do anything! Just look at how you carry your folder with such class..." Mr. Lewis, I believed—that day and today! I always believed you. Thank you for believing in me enough to *act* and select me as head girl over the entire school. I love you, man!

To my eleventh-grade dance teacher (my first dance teacher ever), mentor, and friend, Ms. Paula Knowles. You were so cool. Thank you for investing in the R. M. Bailey dance team. Thanks for loving us and making us feel and know that dancers are special people. Thank you for having a passion for dance—I saw it, and it convinced me to dance. Thank you for kindling the flame in me. You always made me feel that I was the best dancer in the group. Because of your love and acceptance, I am the confident dancer I am today. You will always be a mentor. I love you.

And to all the others who inspired me: friends, families, and foes...you fueled my passion and power, positively and productively, which empowered me to complete the first book (the manual) and rewrite this book. May God bless you.

CONTENTS

FOREWORD

God is no respecter of persons, but He is a respecter of principles! This book is loaded with powerful, practical spiritual principles that are sure to start you on your way toward new life-changing practices. Enjoy the worship experience, the dance stretches, and the health tips, but most of all apply the affirmation, and I guarantee you will launch from dancing for the sake of dancing to dancing with an understanding—with purpose, power, and passion.

It is our pleasure to endorse and support Paulette in her endeavor to fulfill the call of God on her life. This devotional is a part of that destiny.

Paulette has a gift and talent to encourage men and women to worship the Lord through music as well as through dance.

Through this book you will be compelled to examine your level of intimacy with God, and you will be challenged to seek a deeper, more intimate walk using your talents and your love and passion for the arts.

Paulette's desire is to inspire you to worship the Lord more fully. This book can be a wonderful tool to challenge and motivate you to take steps toward being the dancer God has called you to be. (See Psalm 150.) Dare to dance with Him!

—RANDY A. WHITE AND PAULA WHITE
SENIOR PASTORS
WITHOUT WALLS INTERNATIONAL CHURCH
TAMPA, FLORIDA

INTRODUCTION

I am excited to bring you this book. It has been a long time coming. It is a compilation of exactly what worshipers need to grow. I have shared my thoughts on scriptures from a dancer's perspective, including worship words, Hebrew word study, and more. This book includes compilations of the following:

- My insightful devotional with biblical teachings, scripture references, and daily health tips
- Inspirational quotes
- Alphabetized names of God for your daily worship
- Alphabetized thoughts of praise
- Powerful stretches of the day
- Bible reading guide (*with distinctions for beginner, intermediate, and advanced Bible scholars*)
- Hebrew word studies for praise and worship

The need for dynamic dancers in the body of Christ is astounding! The church is crying out for energetic, passionate, anointed, *character-based* dancers who will not wilt or become ineffective in the face of a challenging situation, but call matters as they are—be it the church, the pastor, the saint, or the sinner. Dancers who dare to be different and make a difference…God has the answer to this demand—*you!* God deliberately placed a powerful seed of passion for the dance in your heart before you were even born. And *no one* can stop it but *you!* Your calling to dance with such passion is inescapable, and it is time to reach into your destiny, produce the manifestation, and answer your call. God's grace and greatness are inside of you. God's glory and power are inside of you. Let it be seen and felt.

I have written this book to ignite and strengthen your calling as a dancer and as a worshiper—one who is dynamic in Word and body. This carefully selected collection of quotes, health tips, scriptures, and stretches will inspire you to exercise your right to dance in the spiritual authority that God has given you as well as challenge you to exercise physically as you train for greatness and power in a dynamic life-changing way.

Most of us dancers are extremely busy with classes, ministry, family, school, and so on. Perhaps like me, you find yourself short of time; however, you desire growth as a worshiper. That is where this little book comes in handy—giving gems of wisdom, wit, and encouragement on the subject that is close to your heart.

Mike Murdock says the secret to our success is hidden in our daily routine. *Experts say it takes only thirty days to create a habit (good or bad) and twenty-one days to break one.* So get started *today* on your new habit—reading this book. You will develop spiritual muscle through studying the Word and physical muscle by performing the stretches.

I cannot promise that you will become a skilled dancer or an expert in quoting scriptures. What I can promise you is that if you follow these basic principles and create these new habits, you are bound to win with God! I know this book will give you many practical, creative ideas and exciting choreographies that will come from the depths of your soul, as you get better acquainted with the Lord of the Dance. It will encourage you in your quest to become the excellent anointed dancer God intended you to be—with strong values, a beautiful body, purpose, and vision for your ministry. As you read this book and perform the exercises, expect the seed of passion to be ignited (for some, re-ignited). Expect to create a habit of worshiping all day long. (Worship will become your lifestyle.) Expect to build a strong godly character. Expect strength and tone in your body. Expect your passion to be watered, nurtured, and energized so you are better equipped to touch the lives of others.

Be sure to purchase a *Dare to Dance* journal and keep your journal of nuggets, requests to Him, reflections, and questions. You will be amazed at the change in your life over the next thirty days alone! After thirty days, start the process all over again. By then, you will be in the habit of worshiping, reading the Word, living healthy, and stretching. This is a learning process. You will grow day by day as you practice the practical tips in this book.

Thank you for the privilege of allowing me to invest in your life. I look forward to sharing my thoughts, exercises, and secrets with you as you *dare to dance with Him.*

And So I Dance

AND SO I DANCE BEFORE HIM
Steadfast with ease and grace,
While raindrops of His presence
Fall upon this holy place...
I lift my hands to Heaven
To praise His precious name,
And humbly bow before Him
Forever He shall reign...
I leap to show His mercy
Abound forever more,
And to show my love and gratitude
I kneel gently to the floor.
I twirl with arms open wide
To show that I am free,
And arch my back and face the heavens
To see Him smiling down at me.
And so I dance before Him
With fists to show His might,
And tremble in His presence
For I'm not worthy in His sight.
I dance to show my love and I dance to
tell my story and I declare forevermore,
I will be dancing for His glory...

—STEPHANIE E. PITTSINGER

Before You Begin
Dare-to-Dance Stretch Routines

B efore we begin—I believe that every exercise movement (when done correctly) starts in your center, stays
in your center, and ends in your center. It fosters a
strong center and:

- Allows a dancer to leap higher.
- Allows a gymnast to nail a landing or hold
  a handstand.
- Allows a martial artist to kick through
  blocks and board.

Remember, dancer, you must always remember to hold
your center. Squeeze and breathe. This will help you build
strong abdominal muscles, create power in your midsection,
and avoid mid-age spread. *I cannot stress enough the importance of learning how to move from your center before you
attempt any of the moves in this book.* If you lose the center,
you have lost half the physical benefit of *Dare to Dance With
Him.*

To understand what I am talking about, here are some
simple exercises. I call them my "get ready, warm-up, warm-
ups"—the warm-up before the warm-up!

Your back: lie back on the floor with your knees bent, feet
flat, back slightly arched; focus on the pelvis area and lower
abs, below your belly button. Pull those muscles up and inward (like you are zipping up your pants). This upward and
inward motion will bring the belly toward the spine as well

as lengthen the torso, creating more space between ribs and hips.

Your feet: sometimes my moves require flexed feet. Others require you to point or extend them. When flexing, press through your heels to create length in your body, but keep your toes straight, not curled back toward your spine. When pointing, create length by extending though your big toe, but do not point or overextend by curling toward your arches.

Your neck: do not arch your neck. Whether standing, sitting, or lying in position for an exercise, you want a long neck. Concentrate on lengthening though the crown of your head, and tuck your chin toward your neck slightly.

Your head: do not lead with your chin or allow your shoulders to slouch forwards. Instead, center your head directly above your shoulders. Your ears should feel aligned with your shoulders. To lengthen your spine, imagine a rod from the top of your head through your tailbone.

Your shoulders: often we tend to hunch our shoulders upwards toward our ears. This creates neck tension and constricts proper breathing. You want your shoulders low and drawn back, opening your chest. Think about bringing your shoulder blades back toward your hip. Then roll your shoulders up and back. You should feel your chest open.

You are a puppet: stand with your feet in proper position, with the joint between your big and second toe under your knees. Pull your pelvic muscles up and in, flatten your abs, lengthen through your crown, and relax your shoulder blades down and back. This posture creates great energy. Did you feel it? Good.

Declaration of a Worshiping Dancer

I, _____ , AM NOT JUST A DANCER. I AM A WORSHIPER WHO DANCES.

As a worshiper, I pledge my allegiance to Jesus Christ/ Yeshua, the Messiah, by following His example as my Great High Priest. (See Hebrews 7:24–28.)

As a worshiper, I accept that I am anointed of the Most High God to serve as minister of dance and called as a High Priest, "Holy Unto God." I render to the true and living God, the glory and honor due to His name. (See 2 Corinthians 1:21; 1 Peter 2:5; Psalm 29:2.)

As a worshiper, I endeavor to be a true worshiper, worshiping in spirit and in truth—the truth of who God is. (See John 4:24.)

As a worshiper, I acknowledge that I am called and chosen to let the high praises of God be continually in my mouth. (See Psalm 34:1.)

As a worshiper, I purpose in my heart to be a tither and a giver in obedience to His Word. For I realize that *God responds ONLY to obedience*! (See 1 Samuel 15:22.) So, therefore, even if I sacrifice hours in rehearsals, away from my family, it will not be accepted until my sacrifice of tithe (10% of my earnings) is given in obedience. God does not receive sacrifices from one who has stolen from Him. (See Malachi 3:8–10.) My offering of dance means nothing to Him until I have given Him an offering, that is, time, money, and talent. For I am commanded to give. If not, then I am in direct violation of His Word. (See Luke 6:38.)

As a worshiper, I defy every hindering spirit, refusing to let Satan rob my praise or worship through dance or any other means. I will not allow others to affect my praise and worship. I will praise God as long as there is breath in me. (See Psalm 150:6.)

As a high priest, I take authority over my mind and body by bringing it under the subjection of my Spirit man—the Holy Spirit. (See 2 Corinthians 10:5.) I choose to practice this at all times—even during those times that I do not "feel" like praising God.

As I worship the living God, I will keep in mind the Holy Scriptures that I have learned and memorized. (See Psalm 119:11.)

As a worshiper, I will not be moved by what I see, what I hear, nor feel, but I will stand on 1 Peter 2:9: "[For I am] a chosen generation, a royal priesthood…a peculiar [person (God's own)], that [I] should shew forth the praises of him who hath called [me] out of darkness into his marvellous light" (KJV).

Name: _____

Date: _____

Am I a Worshiper?

Yes, you are. That is one of the reasons you were born, but if you are not walking in the fullness of being a worshiper, you will be after wholeheartedly and sincerely applying the practical steps in this book. This book is more about worship and the worshiper than it is about dance; after all, we are simply worshipers who dance. There are worshipers who sing, worshipers who play musical instruments, worshipers who speak, worshipers who prophesy, and there are worshipers who dance—that is you and me. My heart in writing this book is to help birth worshipers who dance...to take you back to a place where you were created to be...to a place you were familiar with when you were in the portals of glory, a place you knew well before you were born. That place is the presence of the Lord—worshiping Him, just because He is! Worshiping God in that way requires knowledge of who He is, the truth of who He is. That truth only comes from God through the Holy Spirit. That is why John said we *must* worship Him in spirit and truth.

So what is worship? I am so glad you asked. In *The New Strong's Expanded Exhaustive Concordance of the Bible*, one word for worship is *shachah* (7812), defined as "to prostrate, reflex in homage of royalty or God, bow down, obeisance, reverence, fall down, stoop, crouch; the act of bowing down in homage by an inferior before a superior." Another word used is *proskuneo* (4352), "to kiss, like a dog licking his master's face." Webster's also defines worship as *worthship*—"to honor, dignify, reverence, or pay devotion to a deity, religious homage, or veneration. So clearly we see that worship is to show reverence, homage, and honor by acting, either in bowing, falling down, or prostrating oneself. In other words, worship is an action word.

Dancers, you were *created* by God, *chosen* by God, and *called* by God. You were:

- Created to worship.
- Chosen to be a warrior of His royal court.
- Called to minister (work) the gospel. In other words, you were called to *work* for the kingdom.

When you are a worshiper, you will automatically become a warrior and a minister. You will war in the spirit (because we worship in spirit), and you will minister to the one true God.

So today, I dare you, if you have not already—endeavor to become a true worshiper. It begins with action. Show God how much you reverence, honor, respect, and adore Him by bowing and prostrating your heart, mind, body, and soul before Him. *I dare you to worship Him today!* Then expect radical change all around you.

Are you ready for radical change in your life and your situation? Then begin to worship God Jehovah. Here we go...let's proceed to day number one. As you worship your way through the next thirty-one days, God will change your life and the lives of those around you. Get the sin out of your life, and begin your worship *right now!*

DAY 1

Breathe Deeply and Enjoy Life Because It Is Not About You, It Is All About Him!

Who hath saved us, and called us with an holy
calling, not according to our works, but according
to his own purpose and grace, which was given us
in Christ Jesus before the world began.
— 2 TIMOTHY 1:9, KJV

Something to ponder

You see, before you were born, your life and your destiny were planned. For some, that may be a good thing or a bad thing. Personally, I thank God for that. There is no need to try to figure out what to do. All we need to do is check out God's plan for our lives. Will you walk out the plan of God for your life today? Quite often I get this crazy idea that God has given me this gift of dance because He "loves" me. Well, He does love me, but there is a *bigger* purpose for the gift He has given me. The truth is, my gift is *not* even about me. *It is all about Him and for His purpose! It is for His glory and His kingdom's sake!* Now, I realized that no matter how trained I become or ever will become, it is not my skills (technique) or my works (ministry) that persuade my heart toward God. Rather it is the Holy Spirit and passion He placed in me for His purpose through Jesus Christ. He is simply using His gift that He placed in me for His greater purpose, *and* this was decided long ago before I even came on the scene. How foolish of me to think that it was about me. Say it with me, *"It's not about me!"* Ahhh, what a relief! I can stress less...I can enjoy life more because it is not about me and it is all about His purpose being fulfilled through me.

Today's affirmation

> Today, I realize that it is *not* about me. Wow! What a relief! Now I can unleash my tiny perception and open my mind to receive God's greater plan for my life. Amen!
>
> *When you find yourself at a loss for words, go through the alphabet and think of all He is to you—from A to Z. And tell Him about it...*

Being verbal in worship—alphabetized names of God—A

Adonai ~ Advocate ~ Almighty ~ Alpha and Omega ~ Arm of the Lord ~ Ancient of Days ~ Author and Finisher of Our Faith ~ Author of Eternal Life ~ Author of Eternal Salvation

My ABC thoughts toward God

Awesome, astonishing, amazing, Abba, always on time, all right, all that! All that I need, always near, always there for me, absolute truth, admirable, arresting, all inclusive.

Today's health tip: proper breathing

Breathe deeply and enjoy life more. Breathing is a natural, automatic function of the body. But because it is automatic, most people do not inhale or exhale properly. Every breath you take has a great impact on your body because of the oxygen that your bloodstream requires. Learning to breathe properly is not a major or time-consuming matter. In fact, you can begin practicing it this very moment. Just take a deep breath. Inhale as deeply as you can and then exhale it slowly. Do this only once or as many times as you feel comfortable doing it. If you do it only once you have already invigorated your bloodstream with more oxygen than it usually gets. Ideally you should begin your day with deep breathing sessions. But again, don't sweat it by setting up some rigid "breathing schedule" that you will tire of. Just become conscious of it. Some of the benefits of proper breathing are stronger lungs, better mental alertness, and increased energy. Practice proper breathing at all times—when you dance, when you speak, when you are feeling stressed, and when you are scared. Inhale through your nose and exhale slowly through your mouth.

Stretch for the day: proper breathing

Today we will start at step one. Let's develop our breathing technique. Place your hand on your tummy and inhale through your nose allowing yourself to go back slowly. Did your tummy go in or out? If you said *out* then you have inhaled correctly. Now exhale and your tummy should go in because you have just exhaled the air out of your lungs. Your lungs are like balloons, you see. When your fill them with air (inhale) they should swell; when you let that air out (exhale) they should go flat. Now let's inhale and exhale 20 times (each). Now then, increase your inhale power—inhale and squeeze your tummy muscle while you count to 8, then exhale slowly but forcefully through your mouth using your tummy and back muscle. This is your exercise for the day. Practice in your car, at work, at lunch. Practice whenever you remember.

Daily reading

B = Proverb 1; I = Proverbs 1, Psalm 1; A = Proverbs 1, Psalm 1, Romans 12–13 (B = beginning; I = intermediate; A = advanced)

Greek word study

Agalliao—(21; usually translated "rejoice") to jump for joy, to leap, to exult. See Luke 10:21; 1 Peter 1:6; Luke 1:44; Revelation 19:7.

> *It has been said that it takes only 30 days to create a habit (good or bad) and 21 days to break one. Keep going! You can do it!*

DAY 2

You Were Appointed to Accomplish Greatness and Set Apart to Succeed

Before I formed you in the womb I knew you, before
you were born I set you apart; I appointed you as a
prophet to the nations.

—JEREMIAH 1:5

Something to ponder

The Lord of the Dance said, "I knew you...I sanctified (set apart, dedicated) you...I ordained (appointed) you." If you are seeking validation from something or someone—there you have it. Who better to validate you than God Himself? He knows who you are, and He loves you anyway. He knows everything about you, your faults, and insecurities, but He sanctified you anyway. He knows your weaknesses, lack of technical skills, and inabilities, and He ordained you anyway. He ordained you a prophetic dancer and minister of dance...God saw your future before you were born. So there you are! If you were waiting for validation to go forth in dance ministry, now you have it—from the CEO, "El Presidente" Himself. Now then, may I suggest that you forget what others say or think about you? Move forward in your calling as an anointed dancer, prophet, and priest—a King's kid. You *are* who God said you are—set apart, appointed, ordained, prophet to the nations. He has a plan and purpose for you. Now it is time you find it. Enough said!

Today's affirmation

Today I will walk and dance in confidence and authority because God *Himself* has authorized me to do so.

Being verbal in worship—alphabetized names of God—B

Beginning ~ Beloved Son ~ Bread of Life ~ Bread of Heaven ~Blessed ~ Branch

My ABC thoughts toward God

Beautiful, beyond belief, beyond description, beyond words, beggaring description, bountiful, big, big Daddy, bridge over troubled waters, burden-bearer, breathtaking, bravura, bright, brilliant, the best!

Today's health tip: drink lots of water (8 cups or more)

The human body is comprised mostly of water; therefore, it needs sufficient water to function properly. Many major functions of the body are dependent upon water for optimal performance. Water flushes impurities out of your system to promote healthy, glowing skin. As a beauty aid, water keeps your skin supple and moisturized. Practically speaking, drinking the recommended amounts of water will keep your lips moisturized from within and you won't need to buy lip balm! Most experts on health and nutrition believe that eight 8-oz. glasses of water a day is a sufficient amount for most human bodies. I personally drink 5–7 bottles per day. If you are not used to drinking the daily-recommended intake of water, it may not be easy for you at first. Don't sweat it. Just become water conscious, and start by drinking at least one glass of water a day whether you are particularly thirsty or not. Alcohol and sodas have no nutritional value and are counter-productive to good health and beauty. You should work to eliminate them both (if they are a part of your diet). So remember your water today.

Stretch for the day: warm-up stretch with knee sway (great for stretching your back and abs)

A.   Lie on your back with your knees pulled toward your chest. Hold your shins with your hands. Press your abs toward your spine, and allow your lower back to lengthen and widen. Hold the stretch as you inhale and exhale deep, slow breaths.

B.   Now move your hands away from your legs and place them on the floor at shoulder level. Use your abdominal muscles to initiate the move. Slowly lower your legs and bring your knees to the left, as shown, pressing your knees together as you move. Relax and allow your lower back to stretch as you keep your abs pressed toward your spine. Hold the stretch as you inhale and exhale three deep, slow breaths.

C.   Use your abs to pull your knees back to center, and then lower them to the right. Hold the stretch as you inhale and exhale three deep, slow breaths.

Daily reading

B = Proverbs 2; I = Proverbs 2, Psalm 2; A = Proverbs 2, Psalm 2, Romans 8

Hebrew word study

Alaz—(5937; usually translated "exult") to rejoice, to exult, to jump for joy. See Psalm 149:5; 96:11.

It has been said that it takes only 30 days to create a habit (good or bad) and 21 days to break one. Keep going! You can do it!

DAY 3

The Best Is Yet to Come—
Because You Are on His Mind!

*"For I know the plans [thoughts, purpose] I have
for you," declares the* LORD, *"plans to prosper you
and not to harm you, plans to give you hope and
a future."*

—JEREMIAH 29:11

Something to ponder

It is such an assuring fact to know that God knows you and
He is thinking about you. The word *know* in Hebrew is *yada*,
the same word used for intimacy between Adam and Eve. Not
only does He know you intimately, He is thinking *positive,
awesome* thoughts of you today! Guess what? He has already
mapped out your destiny—one filled with peace, hope, happiness, and prosperity. It is God's plan for you. It is up to you
to *believe this and accept it*, then it will manifest in your life.
Many people think there is a great gap separating those who
live ordinary lives and those who live extraordinary ones. The
truth is, there is only a fine line between where you are now
and the next level. Sometimes all it takes is a change of mind
(perception), your attitude, and a small change in daily habits.
Your thoughts, not God's, will determine your responses to
life. You know what He thinks about you. Now what are you
doing about it? I suggest you get with the program and link
up with God's plan for you today! Walk over the line of ordinary and into your future with confidence and hope. Lift your
head high. You already know who you are—now you know

what God has planned for you. Where you have been *does not* equal where you are going as a person or as a dancer. You *are* prosperous. You *are* safe. You *have* peace. You *have* hope. You *are* accepted. You *are* an anointed dancer. The "beeping" you hear is your spirit yearning for more; that is your destiny calling. Click over and answer it. Walk into your destiny! The best awaits you, and the best is yet to come.

Today's affirmation

> If I did not like my yesterday, I can do something *today* to create a better tomorrow. Today I click over to what God has for me in the future. From today on, I expect a superb future—an Ephesians 3:20 future! I focus all my energy on this fact as I put past failures behind me.

Being verbal in worship—alphabetized names of God—C

Captain of Our Salvation ~ Chief Shepherd ~ Christ ~ Consolation ~ Cornerstone, Chief Cornerstone ~ Counselor ~ Creator ~ Comforter

My ABC thoughts toward God

Courteous, compassionate, considerate, Consulate, Captain of my ship, Comforter, Counsel, Counselor.

Today's health tip: stretch before you dance

Regular stretching and correct stretching techniques are vitally important to the dancer. The importance of stretching is also often overlooked. Prestretch and preexercise are as important as the actual stretching exercises; a short warm-up even before you begin stretching is more important. The warm-up (aptly named) warms and wakes up the body a little bit. Simplicity is again the idea when it comes to the warm-up. (Five minutes or so is sufficient, but try to increase as you progress in fitness levels). March in place or do silly freestyle dance moves that you would not allow even your best friend to see you doing. A dancer should always engage in a good stretching session before beginning any exercise or aerobics session, or before dancing. You are more limber and have more flexibility after warming up and stretching, which makes you less likely to cause injury to any part of your body.

Stretch for the day: toe touches (great for hamstrings, hip flexors, inner thighs, and lower back)

With feet spread firmly apart at approximately a 2-foot distance and hands on hips, press navel against spine, then bend from the waist to the floor and touch right foot with left hand.

Come back up, then touch left foot with right hand. Exhale on the way down; inhale as you come up. Repeat ten times.

Today's reading

B = Proverbs 3; I = Proverbs 3, Psalm 3; A = Proverbs 3, Psalm 3, Matthew 26:6–13, Mark 14:3–9, Luke 6:36–50, John 12:1–8

Hebrew word study

Berach or *barak*—(1288) to kneel in adoration, to bless, to kneel down for the purpose of blessing God (from the root word *knee*). See Psalm 95:6; 99:5.

> *It has been said that it takes only 30 days to create a habit (good or bad) and 21 days to break one. Keep going! You can do it!*

DAY 4

No Coupons Accepted...
He Paid the Full Price!
You Are God's Property!

Do you not know that your body is the temple of the Holy Spirit, who is in you, whom you have received from God? You are not your own; you are bought at a price. Therefore honor God with your body.

—1 CORINTHIANS 6:19–20

Something to ponder

Once I comprehended that scripture, a lot of things changed in my life. I feel the same will happen for you. Think about it. God lives in *you*! The same God who spoke to nothing and created everything! The same God who flung "nothing into nothing" and created everything! That is the same One who lives in you. Of all the places, planets, elements, or things He could have chosen, He chose *you*! And because He lives inside you, I suggest you treat your body as such. Remember that your body is not yours. It is God's property! Close your eyes for a moment and imagine this (if you can)... see God inside of you right now. What does He look like? What does He want? How does He feel? With that thought, I ask you, "What would you eat?" "What would you wear?" "What would you say?" "How would you act?" Think about it! Let's honor His house today!

Today's affirmation

> Today I will treat my body as I know God would treat it. I will eat, dress, act, walk, and talk properly and in a godly manner.

Being verbal in worship—alphabetized names of God—D
Dayspring ~ Deliverer ~ Desire of All Nations ~ Door

My ABC thoughts toward God
Daddy, divine, definitely all right, deep, dazzling, Distinctive Delegate

Today's health tip: eat healthy today!
Training yourself to eat properly is no easier than remembering to breathe properly or to drink enough water every day. Snacking on a banana or cluster of grapes is an acquired taste, but it can be done when you understand the benefits of doing so and when your life has a purpose. Becoming the best dancer that you can be is a great purpose and reason to treat your body well. Work to eliminate all fried foods—yes, the onion rings and French fries too. Also eliminate processed foods and junk foods. Begin slowly. Just determine to become food conscious and begin by cutting down on the unhealthy foods. Eventually you will not want to put anything into your wonderful body that is not healthy and nutritious.

As your awareness of health and nutrition grows, I recommend that you begin reading the health and nutrition books that list the properties of individual foods and how their inherent properties affect your body. There are two reasons that people eat. We eat as a matter of survival, and we eat for the pure enjoyment of doing so. Both reasons are acceptable as long as your choice of foods is nutritionally sound. Even if you are naturally slender and never have to worry about gaining weight no matter what you eat, you should still always opt for nutritious foods and well-balanced meals. The human body thrives on the nutrients found in healthy foods, and experiences breakdowns, illnesses, and diseases when deprived of them. Be kind to your body and increase your intake of fruits and vegetables (work toward a minimum of five each day) and decrease your intake of processed foods. Remember God lives in you. Be good to His house.

Stretch for the day: sit up/crunches (great for strengthening your center, your abs, and lower back)

Lie on the floor, body stretched lengthwise. Intertwine fingers and place them at the base of the head just above neck. Inhale, pressing navel against spine; roll upwards. Lift only high enough that shoulder blades are no longer touching the floor. Hold for five seconds or so. Use abdominal muscles (not back) to pull yourself upward and to lower your body back down again. Exhale and return to starting position. It is perfectly OK if you need to tuck your toes underneath a chair or something to keep your feet in place on the floor. If this is too difficult for you at this time, modify the movement by keeping feet together and bringing knees up as shown. Repeat 8 to 10 times. Crunch away the bitterness and release new love!

Today's reading
B = Proverbs 4; I = Proverbs 4, Psalm 4; A = Proverbs 4, Psalm 4, 2 Samuel 6

Hebrew word study
Hierateuma (hee-er-at'-yoo-mah)—(2406) to be a priest—a body of priests consisting of all believers, the whole church, called "a holy priesthood."

It has been said that it takes only 30 days to create a habit (good or bad) and 21 days to break one. Keep going! You can do it!

DAY 5

If There Is Something to Gain and Nothing to Lose by Asking, By All Means, Ask for What You Want

> *This is the confidence we have in approaching God: that if we ask anything according to his will, he hears us. And if we know that he hears us— whatever we ask—we know that we have what we asked of him.*
>
> —1 JOHN 5:14–15

Something to ponder

If Jesus Christ looked at you square in the face and asked, "What do you want, my child?" what would be your reply? Did you have to think about it, or do you already know what you want from Him? If you were not sure what you want God to do for you, how will you know when He blesses you? My reply would be, "Just one moment please while I get my list. I have it all written down. Let me show you my written list." Stop right now and make a list of those things you aspire God to do for you. Be very specific. If you desire to dance under the anointing, ask—then be willing to pay the price for the anointing. If you want a family member saved by December 15ᵗʰ of this year, say so. If you want a seven-bedroom, two-story home with a pool and a fireplace, on the lake, then say so...then be obedient to His Word. For, I have found that His blessing comes through our obedience to His instructions (TORAH). You *must* be very specific! You *must* be obedient!

Today's affirmation

Today I will ask largely, sensibly, and unself-
ishly. I will think big, be big, and ask big...for
I know that my Father wants to give to me in
order to establish His kingdom.

Being verbal in worship—alphabetized names of God—E

Elect of God ~ Everlasting Father ~ Everlasting Life ~ El
Berith ~ El Bethel ~ El Elohe, El Olam ~ El Roi ~ El Haddai ~
Eternal Spirit

My ABC thoughts toward God

Excellent, expert, Eternal Spirit, everything to me, everything I need, enormous, ever-present help in time of need, extraordinary

Today's health tip: get sufficient rest

Get good quality sleep. The body needs sleep to regenerate
itself. Make sleep a priority in your life. Only when the body
sleeps do healing and growth occur. Sleep deprivation is a very
serious condition, yet many people think nothing of skimping
on valuable hours that should be spent sleeping for all sorts
of reasons deemed more important. Studies have shown that
chronic sleep deprivation can be the root cause of many illnesses. When the body is habitually deprived of sleep, it is
measurably weakened and thereby more susceptible to many
diseases. Sleep deprivation can also upset blood sugar levels,
contribute to obesity, and accelerate the aging process. But
even the occasional loss of a good night's sleep has the effect of
impairing mental agility. Sleep deprivation decreases the entire brain's ability to function—most significantly impairing the
areas of the brain responsible for attention, complex planning,

complex mental operations, and judgment. Thousands of automobile accidents annually are attributed to sleep deprivation. Most adults need at least eight hours of sleep a night to function at their best. (See "Risks of Short Sleeping" at www.NBC.com.) Even God rested, so make sleep a priority in your life

My stretch for the day: lunges (great for hip flexors and inner thighs)

Lunges—stand tall with legs and feet parallel. Place hands on hips. Take one big step out with your right foot and lower your left knee as close to the floor as possible in one smooth motion. Return to starting position. Repeat movement, but this time beginning with the left leg. Keep head up at normal angle and keep back straight. Repeat alternate lunges three times on each leg.

Today's reading

B = Proverbs 5; I = Proverbs 5, Psalm 5; A = Proverbs 5, Psalm 5, 2 Corinthians 4–6

Hebrew word study

Cha-gag—(2287) to celebrate, to observe a festival, to march in a sacred procession, to be giddy, to move in a sacred circular dance, to reel to and fro. See Leviticus 23:41; Psalm 42:4.

> *It has been said that it takes only 30 days to create a habit (good or bad) and 21 days to break one. Keep going! You can do it!*

DAY 6

Thoughts Become Words, Words Become Actions, Actions Become Habits, Habits Become Character, and Your Character Becomes Your Destiny!

For as [a man] thinketh in his heart, so is he...
—PROVERBS 23:7, KJV

Something to ponder

You are who Christ says you are. Start confessing it *to-day*! You are a super-duper, anointed dancer. He has given you the power and authority to see the sick healed, those in bondage delivered, and souls changed for His kingdom's sake when you dance. You are beautiful in His sight and the sight of others. You are lovely. You are His special child, and He loves to see you dance. You are a blessing to others when you minister in dance. Say it, think it, know it, and believe it! Let it sink deep in your spirit —now—speak it out loud right now. You will be amazed how your life will change when you think and speak the Word over your life. When you believe it, your whole being will find a way to make it happen. You will become *everything* you think or believe. Do you recall the kindergarten story of *The Little Engine That Could*? Well, it was around the holiday, and all the engines were supposed to take toys to children in the village over the mountain. All the other trains were lined up to take toys to the village. There was a little engine in the group—the littlest of all. He wanted so badly to help. So off they went along the track with all those toys for the excited girls and boys. When the little engine came to the mountainside he realized that his engine was not strong enough to carry him over the top of that big mountain, but he made up in his mind that he would. Notice, I said that he *made up in his mind that he would*! The little engine started saying, "I think I can, I think I can, I think I can." Then he started chanting, "I know I can! I know I can! I know I can!" Before he knew it he was on top of the hill descending to the other side. What he *thought* gave him momentum to do what was necessary. He made it over the mountain that day, and all the children were very happy to have toys that holiday. So you see, most of the results of our lives are the result of what you think, speak, and believe.

Today's affirmation

Starting today I will think positive. I will be positive. I will focus my thoughts on what I *can* do, and I *will* do it! I will *not* allow negative people in my life. I will associate with positive people who believe in me. I will disassociate with *all* negative people in my life.

Being verbal in worship—alphabetized names of God—F

Faithful Witness ~ First and Last ~ First Begotten ~ Forerunner ~ Free Spirit

My ABC thoughts toward God

Father, fantastic, fabulous Free Spirit, faithful Friend, full of love, fun, fourth Man in the fiery furnace, fine, first-rated.

> *It has been said that it takes only 30 days to create a habit (good or bad) and 21 days to break one. Keep going! You can do it!*

Today's health tip: don't eat late

Avoid eating main courses or big meals after 7 p.m. Avoid eating anything after 9 p.m. as a regular habit. Remember at all times to eat in moderation. If you are at a party, hanging out with families and friends, or if you are a short-term guest in someone's home or visiting for the holidays—this rule does not apply!.

Stretch for the day: straight-leg stretch (great for the legs; fully lengthens the hamstrings; targets the entire abdominal region)

A. Lie on your back with knees pulled in toward your chest. Pull your abs toward your spine as you exhale and raise your shoulders from the floor.

B. Extend your right leg toward the ceiling and grab your right calf or ankle with both hands. At the same time, extend left your leg in front of you as shown. Point both feet, drawing both big toes out away from your body.

Inhale and extend your legs so that your right leg is near your chest and your left leg is extended. Be sure to move as you inhale and exhale. Continue to alternate legs, repeating the entire sequence six to eight times. Try percussion breathing if needed.

Today's reading

B = Proverbs 6; I = Proverbs 6, Psalm 6, A = Proverbs 6, Psalm 6

Hebrew word study

Chuwl (2342)—to describe a circle; implies twirling or swirling, twist or whirl in a circular or spiral manner, a circular/ring dance.

> *It has been said that it takes only 30 days to create a habit (good or bad) and 21 days to break one. Keep going! You can do it!*

DAY 7

The Lord Knows Best...He's Got Your Back...Just Trust Him

Trust in the LORD with all your heart and lean not on your own understanding; in all your ways acknowledge him, and He will make your paths straight.

—PROVERBS 3:5

Something to ponder

Sometimes in choreography we think we have it all figured out—all together, the right song, right moves, and so on. It is at these times that I suggest you consult God. Commit and trust everything to Him—your life, dreams, vision, dance routines, dancers, career, children, husband, ministry (His ministry), friends, and enemies. Commit everything to Him, and He will show you how, where, when, and with whom. He will direct you. No matter how trained you are, how many dances you have danced or choreographed—do not trust yourself with God's work. Do not rely solely on your knowledge, skills, or experiences. Ask God to give His input in every area of your life including your dance routines.

Today's affirmation

Today I will trust and commit every area of my life to God!

Being verbal in worship—alphabetized names of God—G

Glory of the Lord ~ God ~ God Blessed ~ Good Shepherd ~ Governor ~ Great High Priest ~ Great I Am ~ Glory ~ Grace

My ABC thoughts toward God

Great, grand, glory, glorious, gleaming, God of grace, Giver, Giver of life, Giver of eternal life, Genius, generous, glittering in glory.

Today's health tip: exercise to tone your body!

It is not a requirement that you become an exercise buff in order to dance. After all, people go out to nightclubs and dance every weekend without having ever exercised a day in their life. But the dancer, as opposed to one who simply dances, has a greater obligation to fulfill. The dancer is obligated to honor her own body with all due diligence and care, and to give forth her best to the art of dancing. That level of excellence is achieved by bringing to the table a well-cared for, finely toned body. A singer tunes his voice with scale exercises. A pianist has tools designed for tuning his piano. The dancer's finely toned body is attained through exercise. The dancer who neglects exercise will definitely be limited in her physical abilities, techniques, style, and endurance. I have mentioned exercise previously; however, today I want to focus on exercise for the sole purpose of toning the body and building muscle. This may or may not include dance or aerobics. I suggest you find a trainer or some professional who can design a program to fit your needs and level of fitness because improper exercise can be more damaging than no exercise at all. Now don't be alarmed by my serious tone, because while exercise and physical fitness are very important matters, the results are also part of the joy of life. I make it a point to enjoy exercising by incorporating cultural music and rhythm into my routines. Exercising can be nearly as much fun as dancing! I think that many resolutions to begin exercising are often discarded after a few sessions because we make it too complicated. Let's keep it simple. Depending on your fitness level, you may choose only two songs (5–10 minutes) to exercise all the way through. That is a sufficient starting point for those new to toning exercises. Those of you accustomed to regular exercise may use more songs for a longer exercise routine (15–30 or 30–45 minutes). I am not talking about aerobic dancing. I am advocating simple toning exercises with rhythm and purpose.

Set out to do this only twice a week for about a month, then increase as advised by your trainer. I could easily set forth an intense, high-powered workout that would leave even seasoned fitness buffs panting, but that is not my purpose. My heart is to help you create a habit so you will strengthen and tone your muscle and that you will not abandon in a few days. I have every confidence that once your body becomes energized through even moderate exercise, you will naturally progress to more rigorous and more frequent exercise programs of your own choosing. Set your body into perpetual motion and have fun with it! My daily stretches will help you. There are different forms of exercising and different target areas. Some forms are *flexibility training* (stretching, or the training of the body to be more flexible to allow for maximum range of motion for all body movements); *strength training* (using weights and repetition to build strong, toned muscles and burn body fat more efficiently); and *endurance training* (training the body to be able to work out for an hour, or dance on stage for an hour). Target areas for exercising might include the cultivation and maintenance of a healthy heart and a healthy respiratory system or weight loss.

Stretch for the day: Hip stretches (great for balance and for opening hip joints, for hips and buttocks).

A. Begin in first position parallel, arms at side. Slightly bend both knees.

B. Cross left ankle over lower right thigh just above the knee as shown. Keeping your back flat and abs engaged slightly, push down to left knee and press toes to maximum point. Breath deeply as your hip joint opens. Hold for 8 slow counts. For more of a challenge, lift right heel—revelé as you hold this pose for 8 counts. Repeat with other leg.

Today's reading
B = Proverbs 7; I = Proverbs 7, Psalm 7; A = Proverbs 7, Psalm 7, Exodus 14–15

Hebrew word study
Alats—(5970) to jump for joy! This not just a verbalization but a demonstration of what is going on inside. See Psalm 5:11.

I Am Like Whom I Worship—A to Z

I am Anointed	2 Corinthians 1:21
I am Blessed	Ephesians 1:3, 3:20
I am Creative	Philippians 4:13
I am Delivered	Romans 7:6
I am an Example	1 Timothy 4:12
I am Faithful	Matthew 25:23
I am Godly	Psalm 4:3
I am an Heir	Romans 8:17
I am an Intercessor	1 Timothy 2:1
I am a Jewel	Malachi 3:17
I am a King	Revelation 1:6
I am a Light	1 Thessalonians 5:5
I am a Minister	Isaiah 61:6
I am a Nation	1 Peter 2:9
I am an Overcomer	Revelation 12:11
I am Perfect	Psalm 18:32
I am Quick Understanding	Isaiah 11:3
I am Royalty	1 Peter 2:9
I am Sanctified	Jude 1
I am a Treasure	Psalm 135:4
I am Upright	Proverbs 1:29
I am Vigilant	1 Timothy 3:2
I am a Watchman (woman)	Psalm 127:1
I am X-ceedingly glad	Matthew 5:12
I am Youthful	Psalm 103:5
I am Zealous	Titus 2:14

I am not just a dancer, I am a minister of the gospel through the arts.

—PAULETTE ROLLE-ALESNIK

DAY 8

If Sin Is a Process, Then Sinning Is a Process Too. It Won't Stop Without Your Help!

With my whole heart I have sought thee: O let me not wander from thy commandments. Thy word have I hid in mine heart, that I might not sin against thee.

—PSALM 119:10–11

Something to ponder

There is a saying in our classroom: "We are not just dancers, we are ministers of the gospel thru the arts." It is our team's motto. This is my prayer over the dancers weekly. Seeing that we are ministers of the gospel, we need to be students of the Word as well. I personally believe that Christian dancers merely imitate (depict) or express words of a song, a piece of music, and so on. The more of the Word you know, the better you can deliver the gospel (message) through movement. Take a preacher for example; one who knows the Word and can rightly divide it will most likely impact his/her congregation and change lives in a more significant way. You are the same way—a dancing preacher, if you will. When the Word is in your heart, it will come forth in your speech, your actions, and your dances. You are like a new computer. What goes in will come out. Studying the Word frequently is only for our betterment. I suggest you become a dancer of the Word. Once you study it, you then apply its principles to your life. Sin becomes less enticing to you ("…that I may not sin against You"). You begin practicing (making a habit of) righteous living. Not only that, when you dance prophetically or spontaneously, your body speaks the Words of God—sometimes it is a new prophetic Word, and other times it is the written scriptures (that are already in you) in action. May I suggest that you become a dancer of the Word? You will be better by it. Your choreography will have deeper meaning. Your movements will have a greater impact. You classroom will have a different environment. Read the Word. Study the Word. Memorize the Word—it will keep you from sinning. *And* you will dance it.

Today's affirmation

Today, I will not just read the Word, I will read, study, and memorize it.

Being verbal in worship—alphabetized names of God—H

Head of the Church ~ Heir of All Things ~ Holy Child ~ Holy One ~ Horn of Salvation ~ Holy Spirit ~ Heavenly Father ~ Holiness

My ABC thoughts toward God

Helper, Heavenly Father, Holy

Today's health tip: take care of your feet. Wear proper dance shoes.

Our feet are important to us—even more so to a dancer! The foot is one of the most crucial parts of the body. There are 200 parts in the human foot. It contains a combination of bones, muscles, ligaments, and tissue that form one of the most flexible and durable structures of your body. The foot is composed of twenty-six bones that function as a spring when you step, and a support when you stand. There are thirty-three joints in your feet, which are connections where bones meet. The foot also contains over 100 ligaments, flexible fiber bands that join bones. Tendons, tough fibers, connect muscles to bones. The muscles move the foot by contracting, which pulls tendons, which in turn moves the connected bone. In fact, all the nerves in your body end in your feet! We rely on our feet for more than we realize. So please take care of your feet. Your foot is an important part of you. If the bones in your feet are out of alignment, so is the rest of you. Eighty-seven percent of the population in the world today suffer from feet problems, thus suffering from other conditions as well. Your feet support the whole of your body whenever you walk or stand. Foot misalignment can lead to other physical problems besides foot pain:[1]

- arch and heel pain
- tired feet and legs
- hip misalignment
- knee pain
- lower back pain
- flat feet

One imprint of your foot tells volumes about you. To take a medical foot test, visit your local "Good Feet" Store. It will tell more than thousands of words. When your feet are healthy, you stand taller and more properly. You have more balance. You will feel better. You perform best with your arch held high. Only you know how your feet feel. God knows how they work! With this information in mind, I cannot stress the importance of wearing proper dance shoes—especially for those long hours of rehearsal.[2]

Stretch for the day: pretzel (great for strengthening the buttocks and opening the hips)

A. Lie on your back with knees bent and arms extended beside you. Lengthen your neck and lift your chin toward the ceiling. Engage abs, raise your right knee, and place your lower right shin on top of your lower left thigh just above the knee.

B. With abs engaged, lift your left knee toward your chest. Reach your hands around your left thigh and your right hand through both legs. Slightly pull your leg closer to your chest. Breathe deeply as your hip relaxes. Hold for 16 counts. Repeat on other side.

Today's reading
B = Proverbs 8; I = Proverbs 8, Psalm 8; A = Proverbs 8, Psalm 8, Revelation 19–21

Hebrew word study
Gil—"spinning around in joy to rejoice." See Zephaniah 3:14.

It has been said that it takes only 30 days to create a habit (good or bad) and 21 days to break one. Keep going! You can do it!

DAY 9

Obeying God Is the Wisest Decision
You Could Ever Make

*The fear of the LORD is the beginning of wisdom:
a good understanding have all they that do his
commandments: his praise endureth for ever.*

—PSALM 111:10, KJV

Something to ponder

As a little girl I had very little fear. I was totally uninhib-
ited. I was stress free. I had fun because I had no clue! I had
no concept of what it meant to fear God or that fearing God
was wisdom. Because of it I got into tons of trouble. If you
dared me, I would do almost anything! I fought anybody that
got in my way. I stole whatever I wanted. I would climb the
tallest trees (with the boys) and jump from the top. I jumped
from house roofs constantly. I could somersault off the dock
in shallow water. Man, I did it all. Thank God drugs were not
readily available in my community back then. I could easily have been labeled a trouble child. However, I was not a
trouble child. I had a great home and wonderful parents. I
was just a fearless child who needed guidance. No one taught
me how to fear, so I did not. I did not fear my parents even
though I got "disciplined" almost every day, I did not fear my
teachers, and I did not fear the spiritual leader in my community. Today, I wish I had...it would have saved me a lot
of grief, heartaches, and "spankings." As I grew up though, I
began to realize the need for accountability and godly fear. I
am thankful God spared my life through all my silly stunts

(many too foolish to mention). My foolishness could have easily caused my death. Even when I committed my life to Christ, I still did not understand the concept of fearing God. Needless to say, I was an extremely unwise young Christian woman. Today, thank God, my spiritual leaders have taught me how to fear God, how to respect authority, and how to be accountable. I realized my foolishness and begun consulting God. I finally realized that my life was *not* Burger King. I could not "have it my way," "do my own thing," "dance my own dance," minister whenever or whatever I felt, wherever I was asked, whenever I felt like it. If I did, I would be saying to the world that I am foolish. In fact, I pray about each dance opportunity. Another way I stayed accountable is by asking my pastor about any and all engagements. At this stage in my walk with God, I am careful to consult with my heavenly Father before I move or make decisions.

Today's affirmation

> Today I ask God for wisdom. I strive to obey
> Him because He is wiser than I am.

Being verbal in worship—alphabetized names of God—I
I AM ~ Image of God ~ Innocent One ~ (Elaha) Illaya

My ABC thoughts toward God
Incredible, inexpressible, incommunicable, implausible, improbable, indescribable, immeasurable, impressive, incandescent, in control, I AM.

> *It has been said that it takes only 30 days to create*
> *a habit (good or bad) and 21 days to break one.*
> *Keep going! You can do it!*

Today's health tip: avoid stressful situations

Experts say avoiding emotionally stressful situations could result in a longer, happier life. Stress affects the physical body in numerous ways. One important way is by stimulating cortisol, which is put out by the adrenal glands located on the top of each of our kidneys. This chemical is secreted normally under acutely stressful conditions for an extra boost to get us through a tough situation or crisis. For example, during surgery the hormone is released. During extreme emotional circumstances it is released, as well. You may have heard stories of mothers lifting entire cars to rescue trapped or harmed children. This strength comes from a huge burst of cortisol from the adrenals. Unfortunately, chronic ongoing stress causes the adrenals to put out all the time. This causes multiple problems, including elevation in blood pressure and heart rate. Cortisol also facilitates the storing of fat and weight gain. Eventually the adrenal glands exhaust, which puts you at risk of damaging your ability to fight infection. I do realize that it is impossible to live in this world completely stress free. Of course we all deal with stress sometimes. However, you need not live in a "state of stress."

Some people live in a state of stress. Like they say in the Bahamas, "Monday is stress! Tuesday is stress! Wednesday is stress! Thursday is stress! Friday is stress! Saturday is stress! Even Sunday, the *only* rest day, is stress!" The devil is a liar! You need not live in that place. If you feel yourself becoming stressed, remember not to "sweat the small stuff." Do not stress about what you cannot control. Take it easy and watch situations unfold on life's stage. Enjoy the play, know that you can do nothing about it, and then move on! Create for yourself a stress reliever phrase. Here is an example of my stress reliever: I normally say, "Okay Paulette, God's in control even though you're not," or "Just let it go, Paulette," or "Just be responsible for your actions," or "Is there something you can do about it? If not, let it go!" Normally with prayer and my "stress relievers," I talk myself into being more calm, stress free and happy. Do not make yourself sick with stress! Just fifteen minutes of exercise twice a day can help to reduce stress.

Stretch for the day: plié (great leg shaper; targets the entire lower body, especially your buttocks and inner thigh calves)

A.   Begin with your arms in second, feet in first. Now tendu to second. Find your center—navel pulled flat toward your spine and leg turned out as shown.

B. With tail bone pointed to the floor, legs turned out, and abs engaged, bend knees slowly as you plié. Lift heels if needed as shown. Use the strength of your abs and inner thigh to bring yourself back to starting position.

Today's reading
B = Proverbs 9; I = Proverbs 9, Psalm 9; A = Proverbs 9, Psalm 9, Revelation 4–6

Hebrew word study
Giyl—(1523) to spin around with violent or sudden emotions (use in context of rejoicing). See Zephaniah 2:17.

> *It has been said that it takes only 30 days to create a habit (good or bad) and 21 days to break one. Keep going! You can do it!*

DAY 10

Created to Praise!

This people have I formed for myself; they shall shew forth [declare] my praise.

—ISAIAH 43:21

Something to ponder

You were created to praise! God chose you to show forth His praises. Of all the beautiful things in this world that He could have chosen, He chose you to declare His praise. What an honor! Once you understand who God is (your very life, your everything), who you are in Him (your purpose), and what He has called you to do (your vision), then and only then will praise and worship become a lifestyle.

Praise and worship can be used in every situation in life. They are a weapon to the warrior, a tool to the minister (worker), and a hassle to the enemy. You can never go wrong when you praise or worship God. When you think about where He has brought you from—praise Him. When you think about how those around you have or are affecting you (be it positive or negative), praise Him. When you think about where He is taking you—His promises, the Word, the vision He has planted inside you— praise Him. You were created to praise Him, at all times and in all situations. It is in you. You cannot escape it. How can you sit there and not praise Him? The very thought that He has kept you sane is enough to praise Him. When you think of how He protects your family, it is enough. When you watch Him stretch your budget week after week to feed your babies, it is enough.

When you see the budding flowers, it is enough. When you feel the rain, it is enough. When you watch the sun set, it is enough. When you see or experience a baby being born, it is enough. When someone smiles at you, it is enough. When you experience the sincere, unconditional love of a child, it is enough. How could you *not* praise Him? My goodness, there are so many reasons why you should. Let's take a praise break right now! Go ahead and praise the Lord, God, Jesus Christ.

Today's affirmation

> Today I realized that I was indeed created to praise God! So I will.

Being verbal in worship—alphabetized names of God—J

Jehovah Jireh ~ Jehovah Nissi ~ Jehovah Rapha ~ Jehovah Shalom ~ Jehovah Shammah ~ Jehovah Tsidkenu ~ Jehovah Tsabbaoth ~ Jehovah Kurious (Lord) ~ Jesus ~ Judge ~ Just ~ Judgement

My ABC thoughts toward God

Judgment, Justifier, just in time, just all right with me

Today's health tip: wash hands regularly

Wash your hands before each meal or before touching your face, food, or drink. We are contaminated with bacteria and viruses from hand-to-mouth contact. You may say, "Oh, I know this, even a kindergarten child knows this." But are you practicing this simple principle daily? Washing hands regularly may save you lots of unnecessary "sick days" and lost energy. A dancer needs lots of energy. Sometimes you find that you are in a place where you cannot wash your hands as needed. In those cases, I suggest you get in the habit of carrying sanitized baby wipes and sanitized hand lotion with you. It is not the same, but it works well.

Stretch for the day: arm, waist swing (great for stretching and strengthening your mid-back and torso)

Standing with legs slightly apart, arms in second, using your arms to twist around, reach arm around to opposite side...and alternate. Do this for 16 counts. Start off slowly then increase the speed and strength of the stretch.

Today's reading

B = Proverbs 10; I = Proverbs 10, Psalm 10; A = Proverbs 10, Psalm 10, Ezekiel 1–2

Hebrew word study

Guwl—(1523) to spin around under the influence of strong emotion; to spin like a top; to rejoice and be glad. Most often translated "rejoice." See Psalm 48:11, 96:11; Isaiah 25:9; 65:18–19.

> *It has been said that it takes only 30 days to create a habit (good or bad) and 21 days to break one. Keep going! You can do it!*

DAY 11

You Were Chosen for Today, Born for Royalty, Called for Holiness

But you are a chosen people, a royal priest-hood, a holy nation, a people belonging to God, that you may declare the praises of him who called you out of darkness into his wonderful light.

—1 PETER 2:9

Something to ponder

Have you ever wondered why God has chosen you? Why He went out of His way to arrange that you are a part of His royal court? Why He insisted on making us a holy nation in spite of who we are? (You are really who you are when you are alone.) Have you ever pondered why He called you His own (peculiar) even when you rejected, refused, and denied Him? And He wants you and me—of all people—to show others who He is. What an honor it is to reveal the spectacular glory and pageantry of an "Awesome Wonder, the King." When a dear friend of mine first explained this scripture to me years ago, I got all excited. *Wow*, was all I could say! You see, I did not understood most of the scriptures back then, but pageantry I did understand. So it clicked for me because I had been in pageants before. I loved the whole ambiance of a beauty pageant. Still do! To know that God wanted to exhibit "His" beauty through me was more than I could comprehend. My friend has since died, and I was honored to be asked to present a dance piece that showed her beauty and the pageantry of our God at her homegoing service. Have you ever pondered about that? If not, think about it...

Today's affirmation

Today I realize that I am special for I was chosen for today, born into royalty, and called to holiness.

Being verbal in worship—alphabetized names of God—K

King ~ King of kings ~ Kurious (Lord) ~ Knowledge

My ABC thoughts toward God

Knowledge, knows my every need

Today's health tip: drink a glass of water before each meal

Earlier, I mentioned the importance of drinking enough water each day. Now I will share with you one of my favorite tips. I drink a glass of water before and after each meal. Drinking a glass of water *before each meal* and 30 minutes *after each meal* allows for proper digestion and prevents the dumping of hydrochloric acid to the stomach. It also makes you feel fuller, thereby tricking the body into eating less. Reflux and gastric diseases are relieved by chewing food until it is almost liquid, and sitting upright for at least 45 minutes after eating and drinking only 2–4 oz. of water. Make it a habit to wait 30–45 minutes after meals before dancing.

Stretch for the day: abs curl (great for strengthening the lower and upper abs as well as increasing the flexibility among the individual vertebrae in your spine)

A.   Lie on your back with your knees bent and feet flat on the floor. Extend your arms so that your hands rest on either side of you.

B.   Exhale as you contract your abs and squeeze your inner thighs together to lift your shoulders up, bringing your ribs closer to your hips. Lift up until your shoulder blades and feet are off the floor. Inhale as you release your shoulders slowly to the floor. Repeat.

Today's reading
B = Proverbs 11; I = Proverbs 11, Psalm 11; A = Proverbs 11, Psalm 11, 2 Kings 3

Hebrew word study
Halal—(1984) to celebrate hilariously, to be clamorously foolish, to rave, to boast, to make a show, to show forth. Root word in *halleluyah* which is translated *halleujah* (literally meaning "to praise the Lord in English)—*Prasie Yah* (Hebrew). In the concordance you will see the word *Yah*—short for Yahweh.

> *It has been said that it takes only 30 days to create*
> *a habit (good or bad) and 21 days to break one.*
> *Keep going! You can do it!*

Think Positive—It Costs No More Than Negative Thinking!

Finally, brothers, whatever is true, whatever is noble, whatever is right, whatever is pure, whatever is lovely, whatever is admirable—if anything is excellent or praiseworthy—think about such things.

—PHILIPPIANS 4:8

Something to ponder

Positive thinking—it even sounds pleasant! Thinking and being positive does not cost you anything, so why not be positive? After all, our thoughts become words, our words become our actions, our actions become habits, our habits become our character, and our character becomes our destiny! Start thinking that you are an awesome, anointed, spirit-filled dancer. Think about all the lives that are touched and changed through your ministry in dance to the Lord. Think it, believe it, *do it!* What you think (dwell, meditate, ponder) about most will become your reality.

Today's affirmation

Today I realize that success is in the moment, so I make every moment count—even in my thought process. I will begin and continue to practice the process of positive thinking.

Being verbal in worship—alphabetized names of God—L

Lawgiver ~ Lamb ~ Leader ~ Life ~ Light of the World ~ Lion of Judah ~ Lord ~ Lord of All

My ABC thoughts toward God

Lord of the Dance, Life, Life Giver, Lover, Life of my head, large and in charge, luxurious, luminous.

Today's health tip: exercise regularly

Earlier, I mentioned exercising to tone your body. However, let me reemphasize the need for regular exercise. If you only exercise during swimsuit season, you are cheating yourself. Develop a regular exercise routine and *stick to it!* Even fifteen minutes in the morning and fifteen minutes in the evening helps. There are simple exercises like walking, running, jogging, and swimming that anyone can do. Try to do something that will keep your heart rate up for at least twenty minutes. Twenty to thirty minutes of physical activity on most days of the week is the recommended time it takes for your body to respond. Regular exercise can also lower risk of cancer and improve cardiovascular function and muscular endurance. Please remember to stretch first. Stretching helps to release tension, improve flexibility, concentration, and posture and relieves joint stiffness. It also builds energy and stamina. Try to include your cardio workout at the end of your workout program. That way, it will burn more calories and it is more effective. Just get moving—you may exercise, you may dance, and you may play and laugh! Just get moving! Here is a simple suggestion: take the stairs instead of the elevator.

Stretch for the day: the angry cat (great for stretching your back and strengthening your abs; one of the best exercises for your torso—front and back).

A.   Get on all fours with your hands under your shoulders and your knees under your hips. Press your navel in toward your spine.

B.   Exhale as you pull your abs up and in toward your spine even more, curling your hipbones down and under, forming the shape of an angry cat or a C with your spine. Scoop and hollow the abs. Hold for 8 slow counts.

Today's reading

B = Proverbs 12; I = Proverbs 12, Psalm 12; A = Proverbs 12, Psalm 12, 1 Kings 19

Hebrew word study

Halijkah—(1979) a procession or march, a caravan; company. See Psalm 68:24.

> *It has been said that it takes only 30 days to create*
> *a habit (good or bad) and 21 days to break one.*
> *Keep going! You can do it!*

DAY 13

When You Are in Harmony With God, Everything You Desire Comes Your Way!

Blessed is the man [champion] that walketh not in the counsel of the ungodly, nor standeth in the way of sinners, nor sitteth in the seat of the scornful. But his delight is in the law of the LORD; and in his law doth he meditate [mentally imaging] day and night...that bringeth forth his fruit in his season...and whatsoever he doeth shall prosper.

—PSALMS 1:1–3, KJV

Something to ponder

A blessed (happy) soul is one who meditates (mental images) on God's Word day and night. Your blessings are tied to your study of the Word of God and your obedience to it. The Word says you maintain happiness when you walk uprightly before God. When you find enjoyment in studying God's Word and obeying His commands, you will be prosperous. Aren't you glad you are studying His Word today? I know I am! The Bible says in Psalm 37:4 that if we delight (give great joy or pleasure) ourselves in Him, He will give us the *very desires* of our hearts—those things you hold dear to you, which you have not shared with anyone. You might even be afraid or ashamed to share them because they are so *big* or they may seem silly to others. It is those things that God desires to give when you commit to study the Word and meditate on Him and His ways with joy and pleasure. There was a time, not too long ago (as a Christian), when I opened my Bible

71

only in church or if someone asked me to. I finally realized that going to church and helping in the ministry did nothing for my spiritual growth. It helped others, but I was still a baby in Christ. Something had to change! I am thankful today that studying the Word is my daily first-fruit offering to God. Our first lady, Pastor Paula, teaches that you should give God the first of everything—time, strength, talent, and possessions. I challenge you to become a dancer filled with the Word of God because what is in you will come out, even through dance. Take the challenge and begin studying the Word today. It will change your dance, your anointing, and your life!

Today's affirmation

> Today I realized that the secrets to my con-
> tinued blessings are in the Word. So I will
> continue to search the Word for the limitless
> promises that God has for me.

Being verbal in worship—alphabetized names of God—M

Messiah ~ Mediator ~ Messenger ~ Mighty God ~ Morning Star ~ Most High God ~ Marvelous One

My ABC thoughts toward God

Might, mighty in power, mighty in battle, mind-boggling, mind-blowing, major league, most important to me, majestic, more than sufficient, more than ample, more than able, more than enough, more than plenty, marvelous, magnificent.

Today's health tip: take some down time

Give yourself some *me* time each week. It's OK, you are not being selfish. Hello! Take a day off —better yet, a week. Yes, you can be sick of stress. Go get a massage, a manicure, and a pedicure. Go the beach or for a long walk—by your-self—or with a friend or your mate. Go play with your dog or have an ice cream—just this once! I promise you won't lose your anointing. God wants you to relax. After all, He did. Read Genesis 2:1–3. God took an entire day off to relax. In fact, He has ordained that day as a holy day—the Sabbath (a day of rest). He commanded that you follow His example and rest. Forget your job, your ministry, the kids, the dogs, and your friends for once. They will be there when you return. Down time also allows time for studying the Word of God!

Stretch for the day: arch shaper (great for your arch and jumps)

A. Stand with arms and legs in second position. Slowly swoop the right arm over your head as you slightly bend the right knee (parallel) and lean into the stretch—toward the right.

B.   For a deeper stretch, lift the right heel and lean into the stretch more. Hold for 30 seconds and switch.

Today's reading

B = Proverbs 13; I = Proverbs 13, Psalm 13; A = Proverbs 13, Psalm 13, 1 Corinthians 13

Hebrew word study

Kamar— to play an instrument, to touch the strings. See Psalm 21:13.

> *It has been said that it takes only 30 days to create a habit (good or bad) and 21 days to break one. Keep going! You can do it!*

DAY 14

Put God First and He Will Put You First!

(For after all these things do the Gentiles seek:) for
your heavenly Father knoweth that ye have need
of all these things. But seek ye first the kingdom
of God, and his righteousness; and all these things
shall be added unto you.

—MATTHEW 6:32–33, KJV

Something to ponder

As a worshiping dancer, you must walk in the reality
that God is first and foremost in every area of your life. That
includes your dances. Years ago, a minister of dance shared
with me the fact that he choreographs only 90 percent of his
dance. He always leaves room for the Holy Spirit, for spon-
taneity, for the prophetic. I tried this and each time I was
pleasantly surprised at what came forth. God always showed
up and moved through me! Sometimes, if I allow Him (you
know my flesh gets in the way at times), He totally changes
the choreography. He conveys different messages than the
ones I had planned...He prophesies, He brings deliverance,
He heals, He saves. Put God first and He will show off in
your life and in your ministry! Believe it or not, He desper-
ately wants to be a part of every area of your life, even the
dance. Jesus wants to be involved in your choreography, song
selections, style of dance, and garments. Ask His opinion
first—"before" you choose a song or choreograph a piece.
It is all about first fruit in the dance. If you seek the things
of God and desire the dance of holiness—rather than your

own—He will bless it. His blessings are for those who ask of Him. So seek God's way of doing things in your dance ministry, at church, at school, on the job, in your business, and in all your relationships. Then the world will see His holiness and righteousness in all your dances. I thought I had a full understanding of that scripture until recently when our pastors taught on "First Fruits" from Leviticus 23 and Romans 11:14–16. It was awesome! I suggest you get the teaching series on "First Fruits."[1] This series will change your life and your concept of truly putting God first. It will change your life, I promise!

Today's affirmation

> I will put Him first *today*! Today I begin to give God my first fruits by seeking Him first each morning and in all areas of my life. I put a demand on my first-fruit blessing!

Being verbal in worship—alphabetized names of God—N
Jehovah Nissi

My ABC thoughts toward God
Never late, never fails, never leave me nor forsake me.

Today's health tip: eat smaller meals, eat less
Eat several (5–6) small (about the size of your hand), frequent meals throughout the day. I do. I love to eat. I love food. In fact, I am known for being hungry all the time. It is not that I am greedy—it is that my body is in the habit of eating often, which makes it hard for me to fast. So whenever I am fasting, you know that it is God! I am a firm believer in eating less, more. Again, I reiterate, I love to eat. I love food. However, I maintain a healthy body weight because I remain

conscious of what I put into my body and how much of it I consume. Normally, what is considered a snack for others is actually a meal for me. It is a known fact that cultures in the Western Hemisphere eat, on average, 3–4 times the normal recommended serving for health maintenance. Today, start eating less—but more. It has worked for me!

Stretch for the day: back twister (great for keeping your back limber and healthy; increases mobility and suppleness of your vertebrae)

Sit with legs extended to front. Cross right over left by bending right knee and placing right foot just beyond left knee. Sit up tall and pull abs in as you inhale and rotate to the right. Use left hand as shown to "gently" pull your thigh. Hold 20–30 seconds while breathing deeply. Repeat on other side with left leg on top.

Today's reading

B = Proverbs 14; I = Proverbs 14, Psalm 14; A = Proverbs 14, Psalm 14, 1 Chronicles 13–16

Hebrew word study

Karar—(3769) to dance and whirl about. See 2 Samuel 6:14.

> *It has been said that it takes only 30 days to create a habit (good or bad) and 21 days to break one. You have just completed 14 consecutive days. That's almost ¾ quarters of the way there! Keep going! You can do it!*

Worship Jesus Christ Through the Scriptures

Jesus in the Old Testament

Genesis	The Beginning
Exodus	Our Guide
Deuteronomy	The Way Out
Leviticus	Our Scapegoat
Numbers	Our Memorial
Joshua	Captain of Hosts
Judges	Our Leader
Ruth	Our Kinsmen Redeemer
1 & 2 Samuel	Seed of Jesse
1 Kings	Our History
2 Kings	Our Power
1 & 2 Chronicles	Our Restoration
Ezra	Chief Master Builder
Nehemiah	Repairer of Bridges and Walls
Esther	The Way Maker
Job	A Faithful Friend
Psalms	Loving Shepherd
Proverbs	The Answer
Ecclesiastes	Meaning for Living
Song of Solomon	Bridegroom
Isaiah	A Given Savior
Jeremiah	Suffering Prophet
Lamentations	Rich in Mercy
Ezekiel	Our Way to God
Daniel	Uncompromising
Hosea	Lover of the Unfaithful
Joel	Essence of Patience
Amos	Our Standard

Obadiah	Our Defense
Jonah	Deliverer
Micah	Fair and Just
Nahum	Our Refuge
Habakkuk	Our Help
Zephaniah	Our Protection
Haggai	A Business Administrator
Zechariah	Our Future
Malachi	Our Priest

Jesus in the New Testament

Matthew	Sower of the Word
Mark	Ransom
Luke	Salvation of Mankind
John	True Vine/Loving Friend
Acts	Head of the Church
Romans	Our Mediator
1 Corinthians	Our Peace
2 Corinthians	Our Reconciliation
Galatians	Liberator
Ephesians	Head of the Body
Philippians	Our Joy During Trials
Colossians	Provider of Our Needs
1 Thessalonians	Soon Coming King
2 Thessalonians	Our Understanding
1 Timothy	Companion of the Youth
2 Timothy	Our Illumination
Titus	Organizer
Philemon	Lover of the Brethren
Hebrews	Messiah
James	Our Example of Obedience

1 Peter	Our Intercessor
2 Peter	Direction for Our Future
1, 2, 3 John	Our Light, Love, and Life
Jude	Our Strength
Revelation	The End

DAY 15

3 Nails + 1 Cross = 4-Given
He Loves You That Much!

The LORD appeared to us in the past, saying: "I have loved you with an everlasting love; I have drawn you with loving-kindness."

—JEREMIAH 31:3

Something to ponder

God loves you. His love for you will never change. It will go on forever, no matter what you do, say, think, or how you act. His love is always the same toward you. Like a master sculptor creating a fine piece of art, he replaced your empty fantasies with a carefully designed life that continues. Has the enemy ever tried to blind you and keep you from the love of God? Well that is his job. But the devil is a liar! He is trying to distort your view of the love of God through damaged relationships, broken promises, and disillusionment. God's love is able to reach you *today*! Despite the deepest pit of your life, He will pull you out of your mess and sit you on solid rock. He is able to heal your heart, even if it has been broken and shattered into a million pieces. Not only is He able, He is ready and willing to right now because He wants so much for you to know that He really does love you.

Today's affirmation

Starting today, I will love more and forgive more because I am loved with an everlasting love.

Being verbal in worship—alphabetized names of God—O
Our Passover ~ Omnipotent ~ Omniscient

My ABC thoughts toward God
Outstanding, over the wall, out of the box, out of the ordinary.

Today's health tip: Forgive more! Love more!
Live your life every day in forgiveness. This may not seem like a medical remedy, but medical experts have proven that bitterness and hatred are the cause of numerous illnesses and conditions. Fear and anxiety causes over thirty diseases. Nine out of ten of all diseases begin in the mind. Fear, anguish, bitterness, discontentment, jealousy, anger: anything that does not stimulate peace stimulates disease! Bitterness, anger, and other negative emotions have been associated with cardiac disorders, glandular problems, high blood pressure, ulcers, and a host of other physical ailments.[1] So, you see, forgiveness frees the soul of the calluses and junk and allows the heart to pump with new life. Choose to forgive today and start loving those who have hurt you. I know it is hard, but it is best. Start today by telling yourself to love, love, love, and love some more!

Stretch for the day: lateral stretch (great for torso and entire lateral side of the body)

A.   Sit with legs extended. Bend left knee, keep left knee turned out, and bring left foot next to your inner right thigh. Sweep your right arm over as you inhale and raise yourself and twist onto your knee as shown. Support your body weight evenly between your right hand and left foot. Reach through your left fingers, feeling the stretch all the way to your fingertips.

B.   Keep left leg in turned-out position. Support the body
on right knee as you stretch the right lateral side. Repeat
entire sequence on other side.

Today's reading

B = Proverbs 15; I = Proverbs 15, Psalm 15; A = Proverbs
15, Psalm 15, 1 Chronicles 17–18

Hebrew word study

Kir-ker—to exalt, leap, spin around with great emotion.
See 2 Samuel 6:14.

> *It has been said that it takes only 30 days to create
> a habit (good or bad) and 21 days to break one.
> Keep going! You can do it!*

DAY 16

Dance Is a Form of Worship That Can Afford Access Into the Holy of Holies

But the hour cometh, and now is, when the true
worshippers shall worship the Father in spirit and
truth; for the Father seeketh such to worship him.
God is a spirit, and they that worship him must
worship him in spirit and in truth.

—JOHN 4:23–24, KJV

Something to ponder

This is one of my favorite scriptures in the entire Bible. How profound this statement is, "Those who worship *must* worship Him in spirit and truth." How do we worship in spirit? Well, first, we must understand what worship is. Worship is showing the Creator our adoration and reverence, and showing His *worth-ship*. It is a spiritual act, an attitude of the heart. When your spirit recognizes who God is or recognizes God moving in a situation, and your heart admires Him, adores Him, respects Him, reverences Him, and trusts Him—that is worship. No one can worship God for you. No one can have a relationship with God for you, but you! In worship, your spirit goes into the presence of God. Dance is a form of worship that can afford access into the holy of holies. Worship is something you do privately. It does not require a physical or secluded location, like your special prayer time does. Rather, it is a secret place you can go into your heart to meet with your Groom, the Most High! When we as believers go into the presence of the Lord, it is an unforgettable experience. When this happens, you are not asking for anything. You are simply enjoying His company, simply spending time with Him personally and intimately. I believe that in order for us to worship Him in truth (the truth of who He is), we must first know who He is.

Today's affirmation

> I now believe that worship is just a change in the heart and attitude. So, beginning today, I change my heart and attitude toward worshiping God in spirit and truth.

Being verbal in worship—alphabetized names of God—P

Prince of Kings ~ Prince of Peace ~ Prophet ~ Power of the Highest

My ABC thoughts toward God

Provider, Prophet, prophesy, perfect, peace, Peace Giver, prominent.

Today's health tip: avoid fast food, coffee, and sodas.

Try to avoid fast food and bad fat. I could write a book on this topic only. Quite often, dancers are on the go and tend to grab a bite to eat at the nearest fast food restaurant. I beg you, organize your day so that you have time to eat healthy, nutritious meals. If not, pack healthy snacks for munching until you can get a full meal. This habit will help reduce the amount of saturated fat in your diet. Also, instead of refined sugar, use raw sugar. Avoid coffee and artificial sweeteners. Use low-fat milk instead of whole milk. Reduce your intake of caffeine, sodium (which causes high blood pressure), sugars, etc. No soda—it has too much sugar, too much caffeine, and too much carbonation. Reduce the amount of saturated fat in your diet. For more detailed information on any of my suggestions, see your doctor.

Stretch for the day: 90-degree hip flexors (great for working on your splits; stretches your hip flexors, which are the muscles that form the buttocks)

From a standing position, take a large step forward with left leg, bending left knee at a 90-degree angle and extending your right leg back, allowing your right shin to rest on the floor (if you can). Sink into this pose, trying to keep both hipbones (headlights) facing forward. You should feel the stretch in your left buttocks and hamstrings. Extend through your torso, flatten your abs toward your spine and reach your arms overhead as shown, feeling the deep stretch through the front of your body, especially your hip flexors. Repeat on the other side.

Today's reading

B = Proverbs 16; I = Proverbs 16, Psalm 16; A = Proverbs 16, Psalm 10, 1 Cor. 22–24

Hebrew word study

Ma-chol or *me-cho-lot* or *ma-chowl*—(4234) a round dance, chowl; whirling practices, as sand. See Jeremiah 31:3; Exodus 15:20; Psalm 30:11.

> *It has been said that it takes only 30 days to create*
> *a habit (good or bad) and 21 days to break one.*
> *Keep going! You can do it!*

DAY 17

I Will Give to God All That I Have—
Body, Mind, and Soul!

*I beseech [beg] you therefore, brethren, by the
mercies of God, that ye present your bodies a living
sacrifice, holy, acceptable unto God, which is your
reasonable service.*

—ROMANS 12:1, KJV

Something to ponder

What an oxymoron—to live, yet die. Often, when the
word *sacrifice* is used in the scriptures it refers to the death
of animals or someone. Yet the apostle Paul tells us that it is
"only reasonable" for us to present our bodies as a sacrifice
unto God. Do you understand the magnitude of his statement? For us to live is to die! You must die to the flesh in
order to be holy unto God. There is no other way! I will be
the first to say that it is not easy. It takes constant attempts
and constant change in our hearts, constant crucifying
the flesh, constant washing our minds in the Word and
daily practices to become a living sacrifice. Honestly, I have
tried and tried and tried. And I have failed and failed and
failed…nevertheless I do not give up. When I give into the
flesh, I repent and again present myself to my God as a living testimony and a living sacrifice. And He does the rest.
What He does is beautiful. And He will do the same with
you. Just give your body over to Him and He will use you.

Today's affirmation

Today I aspire to get to know my Lord in a more intimate way. I know that He desires to know me.

Being verbal in worship—alphabetized names of God—Q
Quail Provider

My ABC thoughts toward God
Quite all right with me...

Today's health tip: take care of your teeth

This is such a personal pet peeve of mine. Dancers, please take care of your gums and teeth. After all, they are the only ones you have. They do not grow back! Try to develop a habit of brushing and flossing after each meal. This could be difficult, seeing that we eat so many meals per day away from home. In that case, take a travel toothbrush and floss with you. Here is a nugget for you, flossing will preserve your teeth more than brushing. You will do both, of course. Be proactive and be mindful to visit your dentist annually for cleaning and oral check up. This will prevent most gum and tooth problems. Remember, dancers, a major part of your presentation in ministry is your facial expressions, especially your smiles. Your smile could add or distract from your ministry. Be sure your mouth is attractive to look at. How wonderful an expression of praise when you see a dancer with the most radiant smile! A beautiful smile alone can capture the soul and leave one spellbound, so value your smile. Take care of your teeth and the entire mouth.

Stretch for the day: hip opener (great for women working on splits; stretching your buttocks, hips, hip flexors (in your pelvis), quadriceps, lower back, and outer thighs. It may feel tight at first, but once you surrender and relax into it, it feels wonderful)

A. Balance on all fours with your knees under your hips and hands under your shoulders. Bring left knee in toward the chest, resting outer left shin and outer left thigh on the floor. Extend your right leg straight back. Bend arms and support your body weight with forearms as your hip opens. Breathe deeply as your hip relaxes.

B. Once your hip opens and your left buttock moves closer to the floor, extend your arms to the sides, placing most of the body weight over your bent leg. Do not try this if you still feel uncomfortable in the basic position. Breathe deeply as your hip relaxes.

C. Caution: If you can, press your navel in against your spine to pull your left buttock as close to the floor as possible. Press through your hands and raise your chest as shown, opening it toward the ceiling. If you are working your abs correctly, you should have very little body weight on your hands. Repeat entire sequence on other side.

Today's reading

B = Proverbs 17; I = Proverbs 17, Psalm 17; A = Proverbs 17, Psalm 17, 1 Chronicles 25–27

Hebrew word study

Machowlah—(4246) a dance done by a group; company dances. See Exodus 15:20; 1 Samuel 21:11, 29:5, 18:6

> *It has been said that it takes only 30 days to create a habit (good or bad) and 21 days to break one. You have just completed day 17. Keep going! You can do it!*

DAY 18

There Is a Dancer in Everyone. Just Watch Babies When They Hear Music.

Let them praise his name in the dance; let them sing praises unto him with the timbrel and harp.
—PSALM 149:3, KJV

Something to ponder

Have you ever pondered about the life of David? David was a dancing man. He was passionate about the dance. He wrote about dance more than anyone else in the scriptures. This really encourages me. I am sure it encourages you, too, because he is one of the most respected and talked about persons to have ever lived. He was also a man of war! He was a man of passion! He was a great King! He was a well-respected leader of his day and even today! Yet David was a man passionate about the dance. Think about that for a moment. Doesn't that encourage you? It does me.

Today's affirmation

Now that I understand that I have been commanded to dance, I will at every opportunity. I will not wait to be asked or to have a platform. I will dance in the street, at school, in the store, anywhere, because I love to dance!

Being verbal in worship—alphabetized names of God—R

Redeemer ~ Resurrection ~ Rock ~ Root of David ~ Rose of Sharon

My ABC thoughts toward God

Redeemer, (my) Rest, Revealer of truth and mysteries, radiant, remarkable, resplendent

Today's health tip: maintain good personal hygiene

This almost goes without saying. However, sometimes it needs to be said. Taking care of your body makes you look good. And when you look good, you will feel good. When you feel good, you respond or act well. When you respond well, you will get good responses, and so on. Excellent personal hygiene from head to toe is important for dancers, especially those on a dance team. Because you share small, enclosed spaces, swap garments, and dance in close proximity—you ought to be aware of your body and its odors. Be considerate to your teammates by using the necessary skin care products. Bathe daily, brush your teeth after each meal, use shoe deodorant, wear anti-perspiration deodorant, scented body lotion, and cologne, if necessary.

Stretch for the day: ballet brush front and side (great for warming up the legs for other stretches; great leg shaper that works the inner, outer, and front thighs)

A. Begin with feet in first position with arms in first as shown. Find your center— navel pulled flat toward your spine and feet turned out.

B. Use the strength in your abs to keep your balance as you inhale and slide the right big toe forward on diagonal. Exhale as you return to starting position.

C. From starting position (see A) use the strength in your abs to keep your balance as you inhale and put your body weight onto your left leg, bend left knee, raise your arms to second position and slide pointed right foot to the side. Try to do this in a fluid motion. Exhale as you return to starting position. Repeat for 30 seconds, then switch to other leg.

Today's reading

B = Proverbs 18; I = Proverbs 18, Psalm 18; A = Proverbs 18, Psalm 18, Numbers 13–14

Hebrew word study

Odah—(3034) from the same root word as *yadah*, which means "to extend your hand." However, there is a plurality in its meaning here. It signifies a lot of extending hands praising and worshiping God (corporate worship). See Psalm 50:14.

> *It has been said that it takes only 30 days to create a habit (good or bad) and 21 days to break one. Keep going! You can do it!*

DAY 19

In This Spiritual Battle, Dance Is a Trajectory to the Freedom in Worship, and a Tambourine Is a Great Tool!

And in every place where the grounded staff shall pass, which the LORD shall lay upon him, it shall be with tabrets [tambourines] and harps: and in battles of shaking will he fight with it.

—ISAIAH 30:32, KJV

Something to ponder

Are you or have you ever been a member of the Armed Forces? Do you know someone in the Armed Forces? If so, you may have an understanding of weapon uses. I do not relate to this personally, but I could at least imagine what it would be like to be trained to carry guns and operate other weapons. I might be wrong, but in my limited knowledge of military armed forces, never would I use the words *battle* and *tambourines and harp* in the same sentence. Yet God said in this passage that He would fight with tambourines and harps. What an oxymoron! But that is how God is—He takes the foolish things to confound the wise. An instrument of praise and worship in the right hands becomes a weapon. Instruments are a major source of weapons in the kingdom of God. In fact, David, Gideon, Saul, and other men of war had the worshipers—who were the singers and musicians—lead them into battle. The tambourine, which is a form of drum, is a powerful tool of warfare. It is a tool that can be used by all ages, sizes, and genders. I believe that the beating of drums invokes God to move. Dancer, arm yourself with a tambourine and make warfare in heavenly places. Go over the line, right into the ene-my's camp and take back all that he has stolen. Amen? Now, let us focus on the harp. In today's society, it is a huge instrument, a rare instrument. But it still remains one of the most melodious and mysterious instruments in an orchestra. David was a harp-playing dancer who made a difference with his harp. In 1 Samuel 16:23 when Saul was being tormented by evil sprits, David played his harp. The playing of the harp by the anointed hands of David caused the evil spirit to leave. *What a powerful word picture.* This validates that an instrument of praise and worship in the right hands can become a weapon. Dancer, I encourage you to use props in your routines. They may mean more than you know to someone in the audience or even to you. If you don't own a tam-bourine, go buy one. I own ten of them—all shapes and sizes. It does not matter if no one else in the ministry of the entire church has one—you get one and make war with it. Have you ever pon-dered why God chooses to point out the tambourines and harp in relations to war? I do not know, but I would venture to say that with these instruments we could do mighty exploits in Jesus' name! Think about it. Imagine using your praise tool such as a tambourine, flags, piano, or harp to fight the enemy.

Today's affirmation

> Today I will do warfare in the dance and with my props. I will take up my tambou-rines, flags, and ribbons to create mighty explosions on the enemy!

Being verbal in worship—alphabetized names of God—S

Savior ~ Shepherd and Bishop of Souls ~ Shiloh ~ Son of God ~ Spirit of Adoption

My ABC thoughts toward God

Sacrifice, splendid, superb, superior, satisfactory, suitable for my every need, stunning, striking, Sparkling Gem, salient, significant, stupendous, super, (my) Shining Star

Today's health tip: kick the smoking habit

Carcinogen in Cigarettes Causes Mutation Linked to Lung Cancer: "NYU School of Medicine researchers report that a chemical in cigarette smoke causes mutations in a gene called RAS that are commonly associated with many human cancers, according to a new study....a direct molecular link between smoking and lung cancer, and the technique used in the study ....are now providing concrete proof that smoking causes lung cancer."[1] Most of us know by now that smoking is bad for you. We have read an article like this one; we read the surgeon general's warning. Whether it is firsthand or secondhand smoke, it is bad for all of us. There are numerous reasons why we should not smoke. The primary reason, however, is that smoking destroys your lungs and causes lung cancer. How can dancers breath properly without healthy lungs? Cedar–Sinai Health System reports that, "Lung cancer is the number one cancer killer among both men and women. One third of all cancer-related deaths in the United States are due to lung cancer. While the number of men who get lung cancer has dropped slightly in recent years, the number of women who get lung cancer has steadily grown. For about 40 years, breast cancer was the leading cause of cancer-related death in women until lung cancer replaced it in 1987. Causes and risk factors: a total of 90% of lung cancer cases are related to smoking. The risk of lung cancer is 30 times greater in smokers than in nonsmokers. This correlates with the total exposure to cigarettes (packs smoked per day times the number of years of smoking, referred to as pack-years). One in seven people who smoke at least two packs per day will die of lung cancer.

Cigar and pipe smoke doubles the risk of developing lung cancer. Between 5,000 to 10,000 Americans develop lung cancer each year from secondhand smoke."[2]

This is a topic that hits home for me because my husband, Joe, was a former smoker. In fact he assisted me with this chapter. He wants to encourage you, dancers, if you are smoking, stop! If you never tried a cigarette or cigar do not! He feels that smoking is a very selfish habit that not only hurts you but those around you. Joe smoked two packs per day for twenty years. Then he quit cold turkey one day when his fourteen-year-old son (out of the blue, or so he thought) asked him one day to watch a documentary about smoking with him. What he saw was enough to jolt him back to reality and caused him to quit that very moment. However, twenty years after he quit smoking, his body was still suffering from the effects. The result: he was diagnosed with bladder cancer and lung disease. Thank God he is now completely healed. Those were just a few long-term effects his doctors said were definitely caused by his smoking. So, if you are a smoker, stop smoking today. Your body is the earthly home for a holy God.

Stretch for the day: relevé plié (great leg shaper; targets the entire lower body, especially your buttocks and inner thigh calves; relevé targets the back of those areas)

Stand in parallel first position, arms at waist, abs pressed flat against your spine (centered). Raise left foot behind your right calf as shown. Using the strength of your abs to keep your balance, inhale and rise onto the ball of right foot as shown. Exhale as you lower. Repeat for 30 seconds, and then repeat entire sequence on left side.

Today's reading

B = Proverbs 19; I = Proverbs 19, Psalm 19; A = Proverbs 19, Psalm 19, 2 Kings 4

Hebrew word study

Pi-zez (pazaz)—(6339) to leap high in the air, to show excitement through leaping, to spring, as if separating the limbs. See 2 Samuel 6:16.

> *It has been said that it takes only 30 days to create a habit (good or bad) and 21 days to break one. Keep going! You can do it!*

DAY 20

Dance Like No One's Watching!

And it was so, that when they that bear the ark of the Lord had gone six paces, he [David] sacrificed oxen and fatlings. And David danced before the Lord with all his might; and David was girded with a linen ephod.

—2 Samuel 6:13

Something to ponder

This is another popular scripture on dance. We all have used this scripture one time or another. We sing about it! We preach about it! We clap about it! We dance about it! Have you ever stopped and wondered or studied why David danced the way he did? David understood true worship. He understood the reverence of being in the presence of an Almighty God! David understood sacrifice! David understood the power of an angry God! David knew fear! The fear of the Lord is the beginning of wisdom. Fear and excitement caused David to worship in dance the way he did. He understood worship to the point that he did not care what others thought. That is the main purpose of my book – to encourage and challenge you to worship Him more fully. Minister with all your might. Go ahead and worship (i.e.: pray, preach, clap, walk, talk, bow, dance) like no one is watching you. David did it and he was king—why can't you?

Today's affirmation

> Today, I will dance like no one's watching. I will dance the dance of reverence and joy.

Being verbal in worship—alphabetized names of God—T
    True Light ~ True Vine ~ Truth ~ The Father ~ The Lord
~ The Son

My ABC thoughts toward God
    True friend, too wonderful for mere words, terrific, tremendous

Today's health tip: consider taking vitamins and supplements
    Many illnesses are related to vitamin deficiencies. Many virtually stem from a lack of vitamins or minerals (or even water) in your system. When the body is depleted in certain areas, you are vulnerable to disease. Make sure you get sufficient vitamins and minerals in your body (such as greens, fruits, and veggies). I suggest you take daily vitamins to help keep your immune system healthy. I have a health-conscious friend whose family uses turmeric (you can buy this spice at your local supermarket or the health food store) on everything (eggs, salads, meats, stews, and soups). Her nutritionist says this is a preventative for Alzheimer's. Growing up, Mom always gave us 1 tsp. of cod liver oil (today they have the fruit flavored ones) daily at breakfast along with a multi-vitamin and vitamin C chewable (250 mg). I still take cod liver oil tablets today. Your body is your tool. You must take care of it. Strong bones and muscles are so important to the dancer. Be sure to include foods that supply your daily calcium so you do not end up with bone density problems. Consult your physician or nutritionist for more ideas on the best nature products for an active body such as a dancer's.

Stretch for the day: triceps workout (great for toning your triceps)

A   Starting in second position, reach both arms up toward the ceiling, bend right and place it at base of neck. Reach across with other arm, grabbing the elbow of the right arm, and pull, pressing shoulders down as you do this. Hold for 10 seconds and pull elbows toward the back. Hold for 10 seconds and switch arms.

Today's reading
B = Proverbs 20; I = Proverbs 20, Psalm 20; A = Proverbs 20, Psalm 20, 1 Samuel 6

Greek word study
Prochorus—(4402) "before the dance" or "leader of the dance." See Acts 6:5.

> *It has been said that it takes only 30 days to create a habit (good or bad) and 21 days to break one. You have just completed day 20. Keep going! You can do it!*

DAY 21

Remember to Put Things Into Perspective

So it is written: "The first man Adam became a living being"; the last Adam, a life-giving spirit. The spiritual did not come first, but the natural, and after that the spiritual....And just as we have borne the likeness of the earthly man, so shall we bear the likeness of the man from heaven.

—1 CORINTHIANS 15:45–49

Something to ponder

Have you ever met people who are so heavenly minded that they are of *no* earthly good? Some of these people say that choreographed dances are not of God. Hello somebody! Let's not be so spiritual that we refuse or neglect practicing our dances. Or worse, we decide not to seek further training. Yes, we can dance prophetically or spontaneously in the Spirit. I have done it. However, God also loves those who take time to study, take care of their bodies, and study the Word for the best way to interpret moves. The Word says that the natural things are first—training, practice, etc.—then pray that God will take care of whatever happens spiritually when you minister your piece. But please be diligent! This will eliminate errors and distractions that hinder the Holy Spirit's work. I would leave a small portion of your routine unchoreographed so the Holy Spirit has His way. I am speaking from my own negative experiences. There were times when God wanted to do something, but I was so focused on what move to make next that I was not able to focus on the voice of God. Those were times when I totally missed it. I danced in the flesh. I am not saying that God cannot choreograph a piece through you on stage. NO. He is the master choreographer, the Lord of the dance. I am saying that if you are confident enough in your moves and in your spirit, you will trust God more. So, practice! Practice! Practice! Then leave the rest up to God. He might use your piece, or He might add His own flare to reflect the image of the heavenly Man.

Today's affirmation

Today, I will do my part in preparing properly (practice, practice, practice) so God can do His part when I am on stage.

Being verbal in worship—alphabetized names of God—U
Understanding

My ABC thoughts toward God
Unbelievable, unimaginable, unthinkable, unspeakable, unutterable, unfathomable understanding Daddy, unusual

Today's health tip: smile
Smile—you will feel better! It takes more energy to frown than to smile. Allow time for fun, relaxation, friends, and family. The world will not stop. I promise! Schedule yourself some smile times. Find a few humorous friends or people. It is good for you. Laughter does the body good like a medicine. Do not worry about a thing; smile about it. After all, smiling is contagious. If you do not believe me, try it today. I double-dog-dare you to smile at the first stranger you meet today and see what happens. I will bet you a dance that he or she will smile back at you. So do it now. Practice it! Look in the mirror right now and *smile*. It is a medical fact that the physical

act of smiling will release endorphins into your bloodstream, making you feel alert and lively. Smiling even makes it easier to breathe through your nose! (tipking.com) Smiling actually conserves energy. It only takes 19 muscles, as opposed to the 47 muscles needed to frown.[1]

Stretch for the day: abs buster/plank (great for working the entire abdominal area as well as your back and sides)

A.   Get in the basic plank position, with your hands under your shoulders and the weight on the balls of your feet.

Pull your navel toward the spine and try to lengthen your body from head to toe. Adjust your feet if needed.

B. Keeping your abs strong and engaged, exhale and slowly bring your right knee in toward your left shoulder.

C. Inhale, return right leg to the starting position, and then exhale and bring your left knee in toward your right shoulder. Repeat the entire sequence for 30 seconds to 1 minute, alternating legs. Do not overdo it!

Today's reading
B = Proverbs 21; I = Proverbs 21, Psalm 21; A = Proverbs 21, Psalm 21, Exodus 33–34

Greek word study
Proskuneo—(4352) to prostrate oneself in worship, to reverence, to adore, to kiss, like a dog licking his master's hand. See Luke 4:8; Revelation 15:4; John 2:24.

It has been said that it takes only 30 days to create a habit (good or bad) and 21 days to break one. You have just completed day 21. Keep going! You can do it!

The Names and Attributes of God

As a worshiper, it is a most rewarding and worshipful experience to study the names and attributes of God, our Father, our Savior, our Friend. The Hebrew Old Testament names of God teach us about His character. All throughout the Old Testament, God slowly revealed Himself to men by His names. Whatever the circumstances, God was there to meet the need, and He still is if we call on Him. The ministudy that follows, if pursued, will completely reward and bless you. It will strengthen and mold your faith and character and move your heart toward Him. May this study chart from the King James version of the Bible lead you to seek Him more, follow Him more closely, and ultimately fall in love with Him more and become a God chaser.

OLD TESTAMENT	NEW TESTAMENT
Jehovah Nissi, *Exodus 17:15*	"The Lord, My Banner", *Hebrews 12:2*
Jehovah Rophi, *Exodus 15:26*	"The Lord Who Heals You", *John 9:1–7*
Jehovah Jireh, *Genesis 22:14*	"The Lord Who Provides", *Matthew 6:33*
Jehovah Tzadekenu (Tsidikenu), *Jeremiah 23:6*	"The Lord, Our Righteousness", *Romans 4:6, 24*
Jehovah Shalom, *Judges 6:24*	"The Lord Is Peace", *John 14:27*
Jehovah Rohi, *Psalm 23:1*	"The Lord, My Shepherd", *John 10:14–15*
Jehovah Adonay, *Psalm 68:20*	The Lord God, "Jehovah Is Lord", *Habakkuk 3:19*
Jehovah Elohim, *Genesis 2:4; 3:9*	"Jehovah Is God", *Genesis 3:9; 2 Samuel 7:22; Psalm 72:18; John 4:6*
Jehovah Sabaoth (Tsebaoth), *2 Samuel 1:3*	"The Lord of Hosts", Jehovah of the Heavenly Armies, *2 Samuel 6:2; Psalm 24:10; Micah 4:4*

OLD TESTAMENT	NEW TESTAMENT
El Chai (Hai), *Deuteronomy 5:25*	"The Living Word", *Revelation 1:18*
El Kanna, *Exodus 20:5*	"The Jealous God", *John 2:13–17*
El Hannun, *Deuteronomy 4:31*	"The Merciful God", *John 8:10–11*
El Abraham Yitzak (Yacov), *Exodus 3:15*	"The God of Abraham, Isaac, and Jacob", *John 8:38–39*

The Old Testament indicates that there are both singular and plural names of God.

Example 1: El—"The Strong One"

El is a singular form. This title occurs approximately 250 times in the Bible. His name, *El*, shows God's character of strength and that He, *El*, is the first cause of everything, as in "the most high God, the possessor, the owner of heaven and earth" (Gen. 14:22).

Example 2: Elohim—"The Almighty"

Elohim is a plural form of *Eloah*, occurring approximately 2,500 times in the Bible. The fact that Hebrew uses a plural form for deity has been taken as an indication of the "trinity" ("three-in-one," from which derives the word *trinity*). The first time this form is used is in Genesis 1:1: "God created the heavens and the earth." The exact form is used with the pronoun *us* (plural) and *image* (singular) in Genesis 1:26. "Let us make man in our image" indicates the mystery of the "tri-unity" of the Godhead from the beginning.

Example 3: Jehovah—"He is the Self-Existing One"

The name *Jehovah* is the most frequently used name. It is used about 6,000 times in the Bible and is translated in many English Bibles as "the Lord" and only occasionally as "Jehovah." In the *Complete Jewish Bible*, an English version by David H. Stern, you will see the original use of the name *Jehovah*. Vowels were added to this Hebrew word—*Yahweh* transliterated to *Jehovah*. It is first used in Genesis 2:4 with *Elohim*: "The Lord God [*Jehovah Elohim*] made..." The name *Jehovah* consists of three time periods coming together in one word: the past, the present, and the future. "He that was and is and is to come..." (Rev. 1:4).

Give Me a Heart Operation, Lord! I Need a New Heart and a New Spirit

> *I will give you a new heart and put a new spirit within you; I will remove from you your heart of stone and give you a heart of flesh. And I will put my Spirit in you and move you to follow my decrees and be careful to keep my laws.*
>
> —EZEKIEL 36:26–27

Something to ponder

It is imperative for you as a worshiper to seek God's will and destiny in all areas of your life— ministry, relationships, and family. In order to do so, you must know God and have His heart, His passion, and His focus. If not, ask Him right now to give you His heart, His spirit, His vision, and His love today. He will do it! Not for your sake, but for His name's sake. Just like the house of Israel in Ezekiel 36—they had done everything wrong. They profaned the great names of God, were disobedient, worshiped idols, and were unclean in their customs, just to name a few. But God said that He would purify them, sanctify them, and bring them back home. He promised to bring them home and clean them up. What an awesome picture of a father's love! He has the same love for you today. He wants to give you a new heart—His heart—and a new spirit—His spirit—hence embracing His will, purpose, and destiny for your life.

Today's affirmation

> Today, with a new heart, I give up the old to embrace the new things God has for me!

Being verbal in worship—alphabetized names of God—V
Vine ~ Vine Bearer

My ABC thoughts toward God
Vine bearing, Vine Keeper, vivacious, Victory Giver, very good, Virtuous Performer

Today's health tip: lift weights to strengthen your muscles

To stay healthy, one needs to *strengthen*, lengthen, and tone the muscles. This keeps the body working smoothly since all the muscles were designed to work together. If you attempt to do something physical that your body is not prepared for (like dance), strain or injuries can result. So, it is important to stretch properly and strengthen your body to stay healthy. I suggest some type of light weight lifting. When lifting weights, muscles push against bone, causing bone density and strengthening. According to personal trainer George LeGrande, use lightweight dumbbells (5–10 lbs.) for upper body toning. For legs, more weight is needed (20+ lbs.). Do not try weight lifting without a personal trainer's advice and direction. Serious damage can be caused by improper weight use or improper form. Please see your doctor before starting any weight lifting program.

Stretch for the day: 90-degree leg lift (great for strengthening your entire rectus and abdomen muscles)

A.   Lie on your back with your head resting back into your fingers, your elbows out to the sides, and your legs extended toward the ceiling, forming a 90-degree angle with your torso.

B. Flatten navel in toward spine, engage abs, and exhale as you curl your hipbones toward your ribs, raising your hands and shoulders. Inhale as you lower your body. Repeat for 30 seconds.

Today's reading
B = Proverbs 22; I = Proverbs 22, Psalm 22, A = Proverbs 22, Psalm 22, Exodus 35–36

Hebrew word study
Ra-kad or *raqad*—(7540) to leap, to skip, to stamp, to spring about wildly with joy. See 2 Chronicles 15:29.

> *It has been said that it takes only 30 days to create*
> *a habit (good or bad) and 21 days to break one.*
> *Congratulations, you have created a new habit!*

DAY 23

Though Made From the Dust You Are Not Dirty. In Fact, in You Is Where Holiness Dwells.

*Know ye not that ye are the temple of God, and
that the Spirit of God dwelleth in you? If any man
defile the temple of God, him shall God destroy;
for the temple of God is holy, which temple ye are.*

—1 CORINTHIANS 3:16–17, KJV

Something to ponder

How do you treat yourself? Is your body well maintained, given nutrients, and kept healthy? Is your mind clear, peaceful, and stimulated with love and happy thoughts? Do you think well of yourself? Do you love yourself? If you do, it manifests on the outside. The very fact that Paul started this verse with a rhetorical question tells us that he assumed the Corinthians already knew that God lived inside of them. I guess they did not. The more we live, the more things remain the same. If Paul lived today he would be appalled to witness what this generation does to the body—the temple of God! He might go insane warning us of the destruction that was sure to come if we continued to denigrate our bodies. Could you imagine Paul? Would he shout in the street? Write endless letters? Advertise on the Goodyear blimp? Or go on CNN? The questions remind today and I ask it of you, "Do you not know that you are the temple of God and the Sprit of God dwells in you?" It is not a rhetorical question. Take a moment to reflect on how you treat your body —God's house—and then answer the question! Do you honor, respect, protect and exercise your body? Or do you devaluate your body? Think about it!

Today's affirmation

Today I will treat my body and mind with respect and honor, knowing that God lives in it.

Being verbal in worship—alphabetized names of God—W

Witness ~ Word of God ~ The Way ~ Wisdom

My ABC thoughts toward God

Wheel in the middle of a wheel, way to eternal life, way to freedom, way to deliverance, way to heaven, way to perfect peace, World Creator, Word, Word of Life, Word of Truth, wonderful

Today's health tip: eat fruit and vegetables

Eat more fresh fruits and vegetables daily. Reduce your sugar intake and eat fruit instead. It is suggested that we eat five or more servings of fruits and vegetables daily. I love fruits and vegetables, but I realize that not everyone does. However, I believe that there is enough produce in your city, island, state, or country for you to find a few that you can enjoy. I suggest you eat fruits separately from your other foods and that you eat your vegetable first. My supplemental program allows me to eat vegetables first thing in the morning before eating anything. This is good for me because it detoxifies my body. Beginning today, endeavor to eat more green, leafy stuff. It can improve your health and may reduce the risk of cancer and other chronic diseases.

*Stretch for the day: forward bend and full body reach (a **great** move; simultaneously stretches and strengthens nearly the entire body)*

A. Starting on all fours with hands under shoulders and knees under hips, pull navel in toward the spine as you exhale and press back through your palms and bring the buttocks close to heels.

B. Bring the balls of feet onto the floor. Keeping navel pressed against spine, inhale and raise tailbone toward the ceiling as you straighten both legs as shown.

C. Now walk your hands back toward toes. Bend knees if you have to, ensuring that tailbone is flat. Tailbone should form a flat line. Engage abs and hold the stretch while taking 3 deep breaths, or for 30 seconds.

D. From position C, press navel toward spine and, starting with lower abs, roll-up— one vertebra at a time. Bring your shoulders, neck, then head up last. Stand with ankles and inner thighs pressed together and abs engaged. Raise arms above head and bring them together again in a temple pose. Point index fingers and press through your index finger to create length in your body. Keep shoulders relaxed through this part of the stretch.

Today's reading

B = Proverbs 23; I = Proverbs 23, Psalm 23; A = Proverbs 23, Psalm 23, Exodus 37–38

Hebrew word study

Ruwa—(7321) to shout, to split the ears with sound, to blow an alarm (associated with trumpets).

> *It has been said that it takes only 30 days to create a habit (good or bad) and 21 days to break one. Congratulations, you have created a new habit. Keep going! You did it!*

DAY 24

You Are Sufficient! So Give Yourself Permission to Succeed in Dance, But Know That It Is Only Done Through Him!

And such trust have we through Christ to God-ward: Not that we are sufficient of ourselves to think any thing as of ourselves; but our sufficiency is of God; Who also hath made us able ministers of the new testament; not of the letter, but of the spirit: for the letter killeth, but the spirit giveth life.

—2 CORINTHIANS 3:4–6, KJV

Something to ponder

I am not "just" a dancer; *I am a minister of the dance and so are you.* God said so! Have you ever realized that everything you desire to do—every move, rhythm, groove, every choreograph, every song is completed with excellence through Christ Jesus? Yes! It is already in you. You have all that you need to be, all that you can be.

So you see, you do not have to dance, dress, walk, talk, or act like someone else. *You are enough all by yourself because your God is an all-sufficient God; sufficiency is from Him.* You are great all by yourself because God has made you great; your greatness is from God. You are powerful all by yourself because the Holy Spirit lives in you; your power is from God. You were ordained to do great and powerful works. The key words here are *through God*, so always remember that. You are sufficient, adequate, plenty, enough through Christ Jesus. Think about it.

Today's affirmation
Today I recognize that God has already called me to be a minister of the dance, so that settles the matter. I will do it well through Him!

Being verbal in worship—alphabetized names of God—X
I found no names of God that started with X, but that does not mean you cannot.

My ABC thoughts toward God
X-tremely awesome, x-tremely merciful, x-tremely compassionate, x-tremely loving

Today's health tip: you are what you eat
Do you believe you are what you eat? Eat healthy and clean daily—make it a lifestyle. Have a balanced diet and be aware of how much you consume. The Bible tells us in Leviticus 23 what we should and should not eat. God calls many foods that are eaten by the average dancers unclean, and He never changes His mind about it. Yes, even after you bless it, it is still unclean because God did not bless it. He cannot bless what He has called unclean. No, I am not saying that eating unclean foods will take away your salvation, grace, or anointing, no! It could, however, make you sick. Then there is the matter of obedience. A few years ago, a medical doctor came to our church and he shared how, at age twenty-nine, he was dying from an unknown illness. Then he got a revelation that what he was eating was making him sick. He began searching the scriptures for a healthier way to eat, and you know what he discovered? He learned that eating God's way, according to Leviticus 23, was the healthiest way to eat. So he reevaluated his life, changed his eating habits, and he was healed. Now he preaches about how he got healed.

The process of developing cancer can begin through stressful lifestyles, lack of exercise, and an excessive intake of sugar, processed foods, hydrogenated fats, and polyunsaturated fats. Healthy dietary, nutritional, and lifestyle habits will help fight against a majority of cancers.

Choose "living foods" such as fresh fruits, vegetables, and whole grains, as opposed to "dead foods" like cakes, pastries, candies, cookies, and most processed foods. When you choose living foods, you choose life![1]

Stretch for the day: lateral tabletop (a great move to stretch the back and legs)

A. Starting with legs and arms in second position, raise left arm as if reaching for the sky, twist slightly to the right, then slowly lean over the right as shown. Flex the right foot for 8 counts, then bring the heel of the right foot onto the floor for 8 counts.

B. Keeping navel pressed against spine, exhale as you relax the back and both arms onto the right leg. Take 3 deep breaths and then try to relax into the position.

C.   Put arms back to original position; keeping navel pressed against the spine and using the abdominal muscles, pull back up to tabletop as in figure B. Then continue all the way as in Figure A. Now switch to other side.

Today's reading
B = Proverbs 24; I = Proverbs 24, Psalm 24; A = Proverbs 24, Psalm 24, Exodus 39–40

Hebrew word study
Shabach—(7623) to praise, to address in a loud voice as in triumph, to shout unto God with a loud, exuberant voice. See Psalm 63:3; 117:1.

> *It has been said that it takes only 30 days to create a habit (good or bad) and 21 days to break one. Keep going! You can do it!*

DAY 25

Excellence Firms Do Not Believe in Excellence, They Believe Only in Constant Improvements and Constant Change!

A wise man will hear, and will increase learning; and a man of understanding shall attain unto wise counsels.

—PROVERBS 1:5, KJV

Something to ponder

It is often said that two heads are better than one. That is why I believe mentorship is extremely important. It is hands-on learning. If you feel you have arrived, and you stop learning, you die! Education is a lifelong process. Have you ever pondered what would happen to civilization if graduating from high school ended our learning for the rest of our lives and we were not allowed to learn any more? WOW! Just look around at the increasing continuing education institutions that cater to adults. After all, most of what I know today I learned in adulthood. If you are not trained in some form of dance style, I encourage you take a few classes, say two years of training. And if you are trained, continue to grow. You may take more advanced classes to sharpen your skills. No matter how much you think you know in dance ministry, you can always learn more. You need a mentor—someone who believes in you. Mentors encourage you despite flaws and mistakes. I strongly believe in mentorship. I have a mentor for every area of my life—my marriage, leadership, finance, business, ministry—you name it. My desire is to continue to grow in all areas of my life, including dance. That should be your desire, too. Think about it. If you do not have a mentor, pray that God will reveal one to you today. Once He does, you must pursue him or her.

Today's affirmation

> In my pursuit of quality and excellence, I will strive for improvement, growth, and constant change.

Being verbal in worship—alphabetized names of God—Y
YHVH ~ Yah ~ Yah-weh ~ Yahweh ~ Yeshua

My ABC thoughts toward God
Youth Renewer, Yeshua, Yah, Yah-weh, Yahweh, Year-Round Friend, My Yielding Point, Yet to Come, Yoke Bearer

Today's health tip: avoid dieting
Diets do not work—kick the habit. Rather, start eating healthy today and always.

Today's reading
B = Proverbs 25; I = Proverbs 25, Psalm 25; A = Proverbs 25, Psalm 25, Jeremiah 31

Stretch for the day: back/shoulder twist (great for stretching back and shoulders)

Stand in a squatting second position, put both arms on knees. Now slowly twist right shoulder toward left knee. Inhale and release. Repeat four times to same side, then switch sides.

Hebrew word study
Shachah—(7812) worship, to prostrate in homage or worship. See Psalm 99:5; 1 Chronicles 16:29; Psalm 22:27.

If you do not have a mentor, pursue one today.

My Mentorship Goals
I will seek positive, godly mentors (people who believe in me more than I believe in myself) for the following areas of my life: 1) dance instructor/minister, 2) spiritual advisor for growth and accountability, and 3) finances and business advisor. I will share dreams and visions with my mentors and allow them to pour into me in order to allow growth in my life. I will communicate with them daily.

Dance mentor, name:

_____

Spiritual mentor, name:

_____

Business and financial mentor, name:

_____

> *It has been said that it takes only 30 days to create a habit (good or bad) and 21 days to break one. Keep going! You can do it!*

DAY 26

You May Be Dust, But You Were Made a Showcase. Show It Off!

But we have this treasure in earthen vessels...
—2 Corinthians 4:7, KJV

Something to ponder

If you have ever felt worthless or could not perceive what great value you are, please take a moment to understand this scripture. Have people ever tried to make you feel less than you should about yourself? The question is this, " Who determines your worth?" "Who decides what your appraisal should be?" The answer is God! He made you to be like Him. You are His precious gem in the earth. You are a vessel of honor to Him. You have treasures inside of you. The word *treasure* used here is the Greek word *thesauros* meaning a "deposit of wealth." It is believed that it refers to the knowledge of the gospel of Christ deposited inside for those who choose to proclaim it. God does not make junk! Hello somebody! If anyone tries to tell you otherwise, kick him out of your life. The devil is a liar and the father of all lies. God made you, and He placed special treasures inside of you, and He loves you the way you are. You *must* start believing that you look like your Father in heaven and you are valuable and extremely talented for that which He has called you. Your treasures will only be released in the proper setting if used in your rightful calling. So know your calling and stick with it, for that is where your treasure, your anointing, lies. Believe that and you are on your way to fulfilling God's destiny for your life.

Today's affirmation

Today I realize that I am designer dust! I am a rare beauty, a deposit of wealth, filled with precious treasures waiting to be discovered and excavated!

Being verbal in worship—alphabetized names of God—Z

Zion ~ Zion's Triumphant

My ABC thoughts toward God

Zion's King

Today's health tip: Be informed! Be wise!

Know your body; know your health! As a dancer, you need to be an informed consumer of any product or medicines that you use. God has given you discernment. Remember, everything in moderation. Be wise.

Be an informed consumer. Read as much as you can about health, nutrition, and wellness. If you have a health condition, be informed about it so you can pray directly about it. Ask your healthcare provider to recommend resources you can trust.[1] Schedule regular medical checkups and screenings. (Prevention is the key to living long and well.) Be aware of disease symptoms. Know when to seek medical care and where to turn if you develop symptoms. *Nuggets:* be safe at work, home, and play. Protect yourself: always wear seat belts and helmets, never drink and drive, wash your hands, watch your relationships, guard your heart, love more, forgive more. Live well, laugh often, and love much. Be informed.

Stretch for the day: high leg kicks (great for strengthening your legs and obtaining higher kicks)

A.   Standing with legs in first position and arms in second, cross left leg over right and kick right leg up as high as you can. Do this for 8 counts/kicks, catching the right leg with right hand. On the eighth, kick. Keep navel pressed against spine, buttock squeezed, and hold for 4–8 counts. Exhale as you slowly release the right leg to the floor. Repeat for four sets then switch to left side.

Today's reading

B = Proverbs 26; I = Proverbs 26, Psalm 26; A = Proverbs 26, Psalm 21, Colossians 1–4

Hebrew word study

Tehillah—literally to sing our praise, give the Lord laud and honor.

> *It has been said that it takes only 30 days to create a habit (good or bad) and 21 days to break one. Keep going! You can do it!*

DAY 27

You Are Marked for Holiness to Deal With Holy Things

And thou shalt make a plate of pure gold, and grave upon it, like the engravings of a signet [seal], HOLINESS TO THE LORD....And it shall be upon Aaron's forehead, that Aaron may bear the iniquity of the holy things...that they may be accepted before the LORD.

—EXODUS 28:36–38, KJV

Something to ponder

Have you ever wondered how you would behave if you had to walk around with a sign on your head that said, "Holy unto the Lord"? How do you think people would behave toward you? Where do you think you would go? What would you do? What would you think? What would others think? How would you feel? How would others feel? Even though you do not see a "visible sign," there is a sign on every believer, and the world sees it. The mere fact that you associate yourself with a man named Jesus Christ makes you marked for holiness. Think about it.

Today's affirmation

Today I realize that as a worshiper, I must wear
the sign of holiness for the entire world to see.

Being verbal in worship—alphabetized names of God—A-E

Abba Father, Beginning, Captain of Our Salvation, Dayspring, Elect God

My ABC thoughts toward God

Now that you have increased your vocabulary toward God, you must run with it. Whatever name you wish to call Him today, go for it. He won't mind.

Abba, awesome, astonishing, beautiful, beyond belief, beyond description, beyond words, courteous, compassionate, considerate, Daddy, divine, definitely all right, excellent, expert, Eternal Spirit, ever present, ever present help in time of need, extraordinary

Today's health tip: Pray! Do it often!

I believe that prayer is the best form of mental exercise there is. People who pray are less stressful and more productive, *so read your Bible and pray every day!* Prayer will help keep you from worrying and being anxious. Do not worry about a thing; pray about it! Fasting is also good for the body. I confess that this is a *big* task for me. Every time, it is a big fight between the Holy Sprit and me. The argument is always the same, "I'm hungry and here's why." On a more serious note, fasting is good for you physically and spiritually. It weakens the body, and it brings us closer to God. In our weakness He is made strong. I suggest you speak with leadership at your church and learn the proper way to fast.

Stretch for the day: cobra (great for strengthening your back and working on your arch)

Lie on back on the floor, body stretched lengthwise. Place both hands beside your chest, elbows toward the ceiling. Press through your hands as you raise your upper body up off the floor as shown. Keep heels and knees together as you press pelvis toward the floor. Hold for 30 seconds. For a more advanced stretch, lift feet toward the ceiling. Hold that position for 30 seconds. Exhale as you release and lower both your feet and arms.

Today's reading

B = Proverbs 27; I = Proverbs 27, Psalm 27; A = Proverbs 27, Psalm 27, Ephesians 1–3

Greek word study

Thriambeuo—(2358) to make acclamatory procession, to conquer, to celebrate a victory, to triumph. See Colossians 2:15.

> *It has been said that it takes only 30 days to create a habit (good or bad) and 21 days to break one. Keep going! You can do it!*

DAY 28

We Behave the Way We Are Dressed!
Dress for Worship!

And thou shalt make a holy [special] garments for Aaron thy brother for glory and beauty...that they may make Aaron's garments to consecrate him, that he may minister unto me in the priest's office.

—EXODUS 28:2–3, KJV

Something to ponder

Have you ever wondered how we will dress in heaven, considering all we will ever do is worship and minister before God? How will we dress for worship? Shouldn't we start practicing now—here on earth? In Exodus 28:2–3, God gave us an idea of how to dress for ministry before Him. I do not know exactly how we will dress in heaven, but I do believe it will be more than our minds have ever imagined. There is "someone" who knows the answer to that question though—it is Satan! Yes, Satan! He was there! He knows the dress code. After all, he was in charge of this whole worship thing. Have you ever seen those fancy shows on TV—the Grammy's, People's Choice, Emmy Awards, and so on? They have the most awesome entertainment and the most gorgeous costumes. Well, think about it...what is the inspiration behind those shows? It is worship! Worship of self, title, and industry, and fans worshiping celebrities. Wherever there is public display of worship, there will be glory and beauty. Well, that is what God desires of us, that we display our adoration, love, and worship for Him in a grandiose, exquisite fashion—in pageantry, style, and flare. Let's dress for worship. If the world can do it for their leader, Satan, we should render 100 percent more for our leader, God! God wants us to dress with glory and beauty that we may minister to Him. Think about it.

Today's affirmation

Starting today, I will invest in beautiful, glorious garments to dance in. I will not rely on my dance leader, pastor, or the church. As a high priest, God has called me to dress beautifully to minister before Him.

Being verbal in worship—alphabetized names of God—F-J

First and Last ~ Glory of the Lord ~ Great High Priest ~ (my) Glory ~ Holy One ~ Holiness ~ I AM ~ Immanuel ~ Jehovah Jireh ~ Jehovah Nissi ~ Jehova Rapha ~ Jehovah Shalom ~ Jehovah Shammah ~ Jehovah Tsidkenu ~ Jehovah Tsabbaoth ~ Jehovah Kurious (Lord)

My ABC thoughts toward God

Now that you have increased your vocabulary toward God, you must run with it. Whatever name you wish to call Him today, go for it. He will not mind.

Father, Faithful Friend, full of love, great, grand, glory, glorious, glittering in glory, Helper, Heavenly Father, holy, incredible, inexpressible, incommunicable, implausible, improbable, indescribable, immeasurable, impressive, incandescent, in control

Today's health tip: good posture

This habit is much too much overlooked and not nearly enough talked about. Sitting, standing, and walking improperly is one of the greatest causes for backaches, neck, and leg injuries. We too often take for granted a child "slouching" without correcting, but in the years to come that child most likely will experience back, neck, or leg problems.

Stooped posture can develop into a hump in the upper back, also known as "dowager's hump." While the cosmetic effects and loss of height (more than 1–2 inches over the years) can be of serious concern, other complications that can occur include:

- Difficulty bending and reaching
- Numbness, tingling, or weakness in the legs or arms
- Pain that ranges from nagging to disabling due to spinal cord or nerve root involvement
- Because the muscles in the chest are shortened as the shoulders hunch forward, flexibility is reduced and lung capacity is diminished, increasing the risk of lung disease.

Spinal fractures can also change abdominal anatomy and result in constipation, abdominal pain, distension, and a reduced appetite.[1]

Let me share with you what happened to me once. One evening while rushing from work to a meeting I stopped to have dinner at Wendy's. A gentleman kept staring at me to the point where I was uncomfortable. Finally he came over and said, "You're a swimmer, aren't you?" "No," I replied, "I'm a gymnast." "Then you must also be a dancer," he said. Finally I asked, "Why are you interrogating me?" He went on to tell me that he was a doctor and he admired the way I sat up straight. In his years of experience he has found that trained swimmers, gymnasts, and dancers tend to sit properly...and that that was a major key to their health longevity.

Stretch for the day: 90-degree side stretch

A. Begin on your left side with both legs extended and toes pointed. Place arms in a comfortable position.

B. Lift left leg at a 90-degree angle while pressing abs toward spine, and leg turned out. Hold for 30 seconds.

C. For a deeper stretch, grab your heel and pull toward your head, extending the leg further. Be sure to engage abs and relax shoulder. Breath deeply and hold for 30 seconds.

Today's reading

B = Proverbs 28; I = Proverbs 28, Psalm 28; A = Proverbs 28, Psalm 28, Ephesians 3–6

Hebrew word study

Towdah—(8426) translated "thanksgiving," an extension of the hands in an offering of thanks, a sacrifice of thanksgiving. See Psalms 95:2, 6; 100:4

> *It has been said that it takes only 30 days to create a habit (good or bad) and 21 days to break one. Keep going! You can do it!*

DAY 29

Watch Out! God Is Training Me
to Be a Warrior

Praise be to the LORD my Rock, who trains my hands for war, my fingers for battle.

—PSALM 144:1

Something to ponder

Why is God training our hands for battle and our fingers for war, if we do not wrestle against flesh and blood? Think about it. In Ephesians 6:12, Paul proclaimed, "For we are not wrestling with flesh and blood [contending only with physical opponents], but against the despotism, against the powers, against the master spirits who are the world rulers of this present darkness, against the spirit forces of wickedness in the heavenly [supernatural] sphere." God is training my hands for battle and fingers for war, and everywhere my foot will tread, He will give it to me. Even though He has given the dance to minister back to Him, to bring glory to His name and to declare His praise, He has also given us the dance as an instrument of warfare. Yes, we can use the dance as a tool of war. We can use our instruments of praise (tambourines, flags, streamers) as tools of war. Second Corinthians teaches us that the weapons of our warfare are not carnal, but they are mighty through God for the pulling down of strongholds. So take your tools of praise and do mighty exploits in the spirit realm. Miriam used her tambourine. David used his slingshot. Moses used his staff (stick). Samson used the jawbone of a donkey. It may not make sense to you, but do it anyway! Take up your weapons for praise and go into intercession. God will do the rest because He promises to train your hands and fingers to war. Go for it! Fight with your flags. Fight with your tambourine. Fight with your scarves and streamers. God has trained you, so go fight. It is not your prop that is anointed, it is your obedience in using the tools that God has given you. It is the anointing of God flowing and His power demonstrating in your life and ministry. God is looking for your obedience.

Today's affirmation

> Today I will use my praise instruments, my hands, and fingers as weapons of war.

Being verbal in worship—alphabetized names of God—K-O

King of kings ~ Knowledge ~ Lord ~ Leader ~ Life ~ Lion of Judah ~ Lord of All ~ Messiah – Mighty God ~ Mighty One ~ Most High God ~ Our Passover ~ Omnipotent ~ Omniscient

My ABC thoughts toward God

Now that you have increased your vocabulary toward God, you must run with it. Whatever name you wish to call Him today, go for it. He will not mind.

Knowledge, know my every need, Lord of the Dance, Life, Life Giver, Lover, Life of My Head, large and in charge, mighty in power, mighty in battle, mind-boggling, mind blowing, majestic, more than sufficient, more than enough, marvelous, magnificent, never late, never fails, outstanding, out of the box, out of the ordinary

Today's health tip: maintain a healthy body weight

It is vitally important to maintain a healthy body weight. Often, we buy into the lie that thinner is better. Thinner is only better if it suits your body frame. God has made your frame to be a certain weight and height. Ascertain what your average body weight should be and maintain it. Following the tips from the previous days should assist you in maintaining the proper body weight. The key word here is *proper.* If you are overweight or underweight, it puts a strain on your organs and can cause premature death and infertility. An improper body weight also puts you at an increased risk for numerous illnesses, including many cancers and heart disease.[1]

Do not strive to be like someone else. Be all that *you* can be! Be your best! You were created to answer a specific call, to perform a special task. No one else on earth is qualified for what God has created you to do. You could be a 007 agent with the right weight and body frame for your generation. *You are the only you there is—the original you!* So, you see, you do not have to dress, walk, talk, get thin, or act like someone else. You are great all by yourself because God has made you great. You are enough all by yourself because your God is an all-sufficient God. You are powerful all by yourself because the Holy Spirit lives in you. You are ordained to do great and powerful works. However, in order to perform greatly and powerfully, you must first recognize your call and your anointing. You must first recognize who you are.

Stretch for the day: forward bend and full body reach up (simultaneously stretches and strengthens nearly the entire body.)

A. Stand with legs apart in parallel second, abs engaged as shown in figure A. Raise arms above head and bring them together again in a temple pose, as shown. Point index fingers and press through to create length in your body. Keep shoulders relaxed through this part of the stretch.

B.   Keeping your abs pressed against your spine, inhale and exhale as you bend to the right, leading with your index fingers. Keep your hipbones level.

C.   Lower right arm to your outer right thigh and reach up and over with right hand, as shown, feeling the deep stretch from your outer left thigh all the way to your fingertips. Inhale as you rise to center, bringing your hands together in a temple pose. Exhale as you bend to the left and complete the sequence. Repeat once more on each side.

Today's reading

B = Proverbs 29; I = Proverbs 29, Psalm 29; A = Proverbs 29, Psalm 29, Philippians 1–4

Hebrew word study

Yadah—(3034) to worship with extended, uplifted hands; to praise; to give thanks. See Psalms 92:2; 119:2; 140:13.

It has been said that it takes only 30 days to create a habit (good or bad) and 21 days to break one. Keep going! You can do it!

DAY 30

You Have Turned My Mourning Into Dancing...and so I Dance!

Thou hast turned for me my mourning into dancing: thou has put off my sackcloth, and girded me with gladness.

—PSALM 30:11, KJV

Something to ponder

Have you ever wondered how some people can go through the most terrible time in life and still have a smile or a prance in their step? I believe it is only because of God. Our Father promises that He will turn your mourning into dancing. What a wonderful statement! One of Webster's definitions for the word *mourn* is: "to feel or express sorrow for something regrettable." If you are in this place I encourage you today to be reminded of this scripture. In fact, I encourage you to dance before the Lord right now. As you focus on God, minister to Him. As you turn your eyes on what He has already done for you, your mourning will pale in comparison to what He has done. Remember that this too will past. So dance with all your heart, soul, and mind—with all your energy before the Lord of the Dance. He promised to turn your sorrow for something regrettable. (See Psalm 30:11.) into dancing. Of all the things that God could have turned our mourning into, He chose dancing. Dancing must be important to God. I believe it is...and you are important to Him, too. In fact, He promised to take off your sackcloth (mourning clothes) and cloth you with gladness (shining, smooth by pleasure, joy, happiness, pleased). What an awesome promise!

Today's affirmation

Today I thank you, Lord, for turning my mourning into dancing. In the midst of mourning I will remember your promise.

Being verbal in worship—alphabetized names of God—P-T

Prince of Kings ~ Prince of Peace ~ Prophet ~ Power of the Highest ~ Quail Provider ~ Redeemer ~ Resurrection ~ Rock ~ Root of David ~ Rose of Sharon ~ Savior ~ Shepherd and Bishop of Souls ~ Shiloh ~ Son of God ~ Spirit of Adoption ~ True Light ~ True Vine ~ Truth ~ The Father ~ The Lord ~ The Son

Today's health tip: take care of your face

Your face is the first thing people see and the first thing they are most likely to remember after the initial encounter, so take care of it. Your skin is the largest organ in your body. The skin on your face is one of the most delicate parts of you. It is your face that gets exposed to sun all day long; gets oily or dry due to weather changes; gets rubbed, scrubbed, and patted after each wash; gets pinched, pulled, pushed, slapped, and covered in make-up day in and day out; that wears most of your expressions. Your face is a major part of you. It is like your signature—whether it is your smile, your white teeth, your deep sparkling eyes, your wink, those lashes, your cute ears—it is all a part of your face. Give the best impression by taking good care of your face. Always wash and moisture your face properly. I cannot emphasize the importance of moisturizing. No matter how young or old you are, moisturize after each wash. Use proper cleansing and moisturizing products. Do not scrub your face with a towel after washing it; instead pat it dry. This is less rough. Have occasional facials. If you have acne problems (like I do), pray about what products to use, then see a dermatologist right away.

Stretch for the circles (great move for inner and outer thighs; teaches y to stabilize your abs and hips during circular move

A.   Lie back, arms at your sides, knees bent and feet
     flat floor. Extend right leg and point toes as shown.
     Ex tighten abs, navel in. press spine downward.

B ly circle right leg counterclockwise, as shown, mak-
  sure to keep hips level and motionless. Inhale as you
  le leg outward, away from body. Exhale as you circle
  vard, toward the body. After circling 4 – 8 times in

that direction, switch to clockwise fo ore circles.
Repeat this sequence with the other l

Today's reading

B = Proverbs 30; I = Proverbs 30, Psalm 3 roverbs
30, Psalm 30, 1 Corinthians 1–3

Hebrew word study

Yah-gil—God dances in joy over you; *Ya* "God";
gil means "dances."

CONGRATULATIONS! YOU DID IT. You created a habit of studying the Word, praising and worshiping God in your own way, pursuing a healthier life; you now know numerous Hebrew words for *dance.* You have strengthened and conditioned your body through the stretches, you have renewed your mind and ignited the soul, and you have enjoyed the worship experience with your Father, I am sure! You have applied the affirmations. I am so proud of you. You are on your way toward new, life-changing practices. I pray that you continue in them. If you do, I guarantee that you will launch from dancing for the sake of dancing to dancing with an understanding—with purpose, power, and passion. I encourage you to document every experience you have had while going through this book. Document everything— the Words/prophecies that God has spoken to you, those carpet experiences you have had, those onion-peeling moments— when you faced yourself and dealt with the issues you had, but it brought about change. Document the pain you have experienced from the stretches; make a journal.

God is no respecter of persons, but He is a respecter of principles. He will honor what you have committed to. Commit your ways to the Lord. *Enough is enough!* It is time you dare to dance like no one is watching. This was your call to action to a new level of training and experiences. Remember you can reread this book. As you have experienced for yourself, it is a wonderful tool filled with daily, life-changing habits—all to challenge and motivate you to take small, daily action steps toward being the person God has called you to be. He has ordained you to dance (Psalm 150), so *dare to dance with Him.*

DAY 31

Dancers Are Predestined, Called, Justified, and Glorified!

Moreover whom he did predestinate, them he also called: and whom he called them he also justified: and whom he justified, them he also glorified.
—ROMANS 8:30, KJV

Something to ponder

This is our last day together. Thank you for spending the last thirty-one days with me and allowing me to pour into your life. As we wrap up, let me encourage you that everything you have read in the Word is true. Every promise is for you; you are called! You have the authority through Jesus Christ. You are affirmed. You are an awesome, anointed dancer. Now walk in that authority *today*. You have the Holy Spirit inside to guide you, to teach you, to dance with you…you can do this. I know you can. You will dance under such a strong anointing that demons will flee, souls will be saved, lives will be changed, and the sick will be healed. Yes you can do this. It says in the Book of Romans that those whom God Himself predestined, He also called. If you know without a shadow of a doubt that you are called to dance ministry, then believe also that you are justified, which in Hebrew is from the root word *Ge'eh* (gay-eh), meaning "to mount up," "to rise," "to be majestic," "triumph gloriously." Dancer, know that God had you on His mind before the foundation of the world. And even then He trusted you to be who you are. You are predestined to dance; you are called to dance; you are justified to dance; you are glorified to dance! Now, I am not trying to inflate your ego, but that is what the Word said about you. What more affirmation do you need? Step out and step up in your dance. Be excellent. And dance like no one is watching you. I dare you; no, I double dog dare you to dance with Him…and see how your life will radically change.

Today's affirmation

> Today I realized that I am predestined, called, justified, and glorified to do what God has for me to do, so I will walk in the authority of knowing who I am and whose I am!

Being verbal in worship—alphabetized names of God—U-Z

Understanding ~ The Vine ~ Vine Bearer ~ Witness ~ Word of God ~ The Way ~ Wisdom ~ Yahweh ~ Yeshua ~ Zion's Trumpet

Today's health tip: live a well-balanced life

The motto for our home is, "Live well, laugh often, and love much!" Allow time for relaxation; do not build up a sleep debt by not sleeping long enough; do not worry about a thing. All things in balance in every area of your life, even dance! You are made up of body, mind/spirit, and soul, and each one is as important as the other. Otherwise God would not have made it. Take care for your body through proper diet and exercise. Working (your job) is an essential part of body maintenance. Take care of your mind by choosing positive thoughts about yourself and others. Be careful what you allow in your mind, for "as a man/woman thinks so is he/she" (Prov. 23:7). Read, play, and relax— they are all equally important for the mind. Take care of your soul. This is a once-in-a-lifetime decision, and then God takes over. Once you commit your soul, your life to Him, He protects it from the enemy and saves you from an eternity in hell. Have a balanced life. Do not get caught up in the rat race of going to church every time the doors open. Do not allow "religious stuff" to take you off balance. Do not allow church to take over your life. Do not allow ministry to ruin your life. That is not God, for my God is a God of order and balance, and He has established the end from the beginning. In the end we shall find eternal peace and rest. That was already completed, then He backed up and made time for your sake; even in your time He established a day of rest. Therefore, do not let your family, the job, ministry, or church to burn you out, and then blame God. Remember the advice of the wise karate master, Mr. Miyagi, from the movie *Karate Kid?* Regarding balance he said, "Lesson not just karate only, lesson for whole life. Whole life have a balance, everything better. Understand?" I encourage you to make every effort in living a well-balanced life. Starting today, take an inventory of how you spend your time—body, mind (spirit), and soul. If you discover that you are out of alignment, bring balance to all areas of your life *today.* Live well, laugh often, and love much!

Stretch for the day: glutes lifter (great for the glutes; this is the muscle that forms the buttocks)

A.   Lie face down, arm under chin. Breathe deeply and relax. Lift left lower leg toward the ceiling, toes pointed as shown.

B.   Now lift the upper left leg from the pelvis while extending lower leg toward the ceiling and pressing pelvis toward the floor. Hold position for 30 seconds. Repeat with right leg.

Today's reading

B = Proverbs 31; I = Proverbs 31, Psalm 31; A = Proverbs 31, Psalm 31, 1 Corinthians 9

Hebrew word study

Tac-wdah—to clap your hands with excitement.

> *It has been said that it takes only 30 days to create a habit (good or bad) and 21 days to break one. Congratulations, you have practiced a new habit for thirty days plus one! You did it!*

The Dancer's 31 Days of Worship as a Lifestyle Devotional Guide

Experts say it takes 30 days to create a habit and 21 days to break one.

Daily guide for praise and worship: praise for at least 10 minutes; worship for at least 10 minutes.

Daily guide for prayer: B = Beginner (10 min.); I = Intermediate (1 hr.); A = Advanced (3 hrs. or more).

Beginning Reading Schedule

Day 1	Psalm 1			
Day 2	Psalm 2			
Day 3	Psalm 3			
Day 4	Psalm 4			
Day 5	Psalm 5			
Day 6	Psalm 6			
Day 7	Psalm 7			
Day 8	Psalm 8			
Day 9	Psalm 9			
Day 10	Psalm 10			
Day 11	Psalm 11			
Day 12	Psalm 12			
Day 13	Psalm 13			

Day 14	Psalm 14			
Day 15	Psalm 15			
Day 16	Psalm 16			
Day 17	Psalm 17			
Day 18	Psalm 18			
Day 19	Psalm 19			
Day 20	Psalm 20			
Day 21	Psalm 21			
Day 22	Psalm 22			
Day 23	Psalm 23			
Day 24	Psalm 24			
Day 25	Psalm 25			
Day 26	Psalm 26			
Day 27	Psalm 27			
Day 28	Psalm 28			
Day 29	Psalm 29			
Day 30	Psalm 30			
Day 31	Psalm 31			

The Dancer's 31 Days of Worship as a Lifestyle Devotional Guide

Experts say it takes 30 days to create a habit and 21 days to break one.

Daily guide for praise and worship: praise for at least 10 minutes; worship for at least 10 minutes.

Daily guide for prayer: B = Beginner (10 min.); I = Intermediate (1 hr.); A = Advanced (3 hrs. or more).

Intermediate Reading Schedule

Day 1	Psalm 1	Proverbs 1		
Day 2	Psalm 2	Proverbs 2		
Day 3	Psalm 3	Proverbs 3		
Day 4	Psalm 4	Proverbs 4		
Day 5	Psalm 5	Proverbs 5		
Day 6	Psalm 6	Proverbs 6		
Day 7	Psalm 7	Proverbs 7		
Day 8	Psalm 8	Proverbs 8		
Day 9	Psalm 9	Proverbs 9		
Day 10	Psalm 10	Proverbs 10		
Day 11	Psalm 11	Proverbs 11		
Day 12	Psalm 12	Proverbs 12		
Day 13	Psalm 13	Proverbs 13		
Day 14	Psalm 14	Proverbs 14		

Day 15	Psalm 15	Proverbs 15		
Day 16	Psalm 16	Proverbs 16		
Day 17	Psalm 17	Proverbs 17		
Day 18	Psalm 18	Proverbs 18		
Day 19	Psalm 19	Proverbs 19		
Day 20	Psalm 20	Proverbs 20		
Day 21	Psalm 21	Proverbs 21		
Day 22	Psalm 22	Proverbs 22		
Day 23	Psalm 23	Proverbs 23		
Day 24	Psalm 24	Proverbs 24		
Day 25	Psalm 25	Proverbs 25		
Day 26	Psalm 26	Proverbs 26		
Day 27	Psalm 27	Proverbs 27		
Day 28	Psalm 28	Proverbs 28		
Day 29	Psalm 29	Proverbs 29		
Day 30	Psalm 30	Proverbs 30		
Day 31	Psalm 31	Proverbs 31		

The Dancer's 31 Days of Worship as a Lifestyle Devotional Guide

Experts say it takes 30 days to create a habit and 21 days to break one.

Daily guide for praise and worship: praise for at least 10 minutes; worship for at least 10 minutes.

Daily guide for prayer: B = Beginner (10 min.); I = Intermediate (1 hr.); A = Advanced (3 hrs. or more).

Advanced Reading Schedule

Day 1	Psalm 1	Proverbs 1	Romans 12–13	
Day 2	Psalm 2	Proverbs 2	Romans 8	
Day 3	Psalm 3	Proverbs 3	Matthew 26:6–13; Mark 14:3–9; Luke 6:36–50; John 12:1–8	
Day 4	Psalm 4	Proverbs 4	2 Samuel 6	
Day 5	Psalm 5	Proverbs 5	2 Corinthians 4–6	
Day 6	Psalm 6	Proverbs 6	2 Samuel 23	
Day 7	Psalm 7	Proverbs 7	Exodus 14–15	
Day 8	Psalms 8	Proverbs 8	Revelation 19–21	
Day 9	Psalm 9	Proverbs 9	Revelation 4–6	
Day 10	Psalm 10	Proverbs 10	Ezekiel 1–2	
Day 11	Psalm 11	Proverbs 11	2 Kings 3	
Day 12	Psalm 12	Proverbs 12	1 Kings 19	
Day 13	Psalm 13	Proverbs 13	1 Corinthians 13	

Day 14	Psalm 14	Proverbs 14	1 Corinthians 13–16
Day 15	Psalm 15	Proverbs 15	1 Corinthians 17–18
Day 16	Psalm 16	Proverbs 16	1 Corinthians 22–24
Day 17	Psalm 17	Proverbs 17	1 Corinthians 25–27
Day 18	Psalm 18	Proverbs 18	Numbers 13–14
Day 19	Psalm 19	Proverbs 19	2 Kings 4
Day 20	Psalm 20	Proverbs 20	1 Samuel 6
Day 21	Psalm 21	Proverbs 21	Exodus 33–34
Day 22	Psalm 22	Proverbs 22	Exodus 35–36
Day 23	Psalm 23	Proverbs 23	Exodus 37–38
Day 24	Psalm 24	Proverbs 24	Exodus 39–40
Day 25	Psalm 25	Proverbs 25	Jeremiah 31
Day 26	Psalm 26	Proverbs 26	Colossians 1–4
Day 27	Psalm 27	Proverbs 27	Ephesians 1–3
Day 28	Psalm 28	Proverbs 28	Ephesians 3–6
Day 29	Psalm 29	Proverbs 29	Philippians 1
Day 30	Psalm 30	Proverbs 30	1 Corinthians 1–2
Day 31	Psalm 31	Proverbs 31	1 Corinthians 9

NOTES

Day 8

1. Dr. Foot's Health Information, "Foot Anatomy," www .drfoot.com.

2. For a list of dance shoes, visit www.dancewear.com.

Day 14

1. Call (813) 879-HOPE or visit www.paulawhite.org and ask for the Paula White series on First Fruits.

Day 15

1. For more information see Life Application Ministries, mindsync.com and http://www.geocities.com/bongoosie /Miscellaneous1/forgiveness.html.

Day 19

1. See www.sciencedaily.com, Oct. 17, 2002.

2. See www.cedar-sinai.edu.

Day 21

1. See www.tipking.com and http://www.angelfire.com /il/offthewall98/Yearone/Issue3/Smiling.html, Smiling by DragonSlayer.

Day 24

1. See www.drcolbert.com.

Day 26

1. For more information visit www.4women.gov.

Day 28

1. See Yahoo Health at www.yahoo.com, "Posture: Complications" provided by ISL Consulting Co.

Day 29

1. For more information see http://www.ucdmc.ucdavis.edu /ucdhs/health/az/ 53WeightControl /doc53severity.html.

The companion workbook and journal to *Dare to Dance With Him* is available from:

DARE TO DANCE, INC.

P.O. Box 24492

Tampa, FL 33623

www.daretodance.org

Coming in Spring 2005: *Dare to Dance Bible Study Guide*, book on CD, calendar, and day planner.